IMPACT BEYOND THE GAME

IMPACT BEYOND THE GAME

HOW ATHLETES CAN BUILD INFLUENCE, MONETIZE THEIR BRAND, AND CREATE A LEGACY

MALCOLM LEMMONS

PROLIFIC
P U B L I S H I N G

IMPACT BEYOND THE GAME

How Athletes Can Build Influence, Monetize Their Brand, and Create a Legacy

ISBN   978-1-5445-0737-8 *Hardcover*

978-1-5445-0736-1 *Paperback*

978-1-5445-0735-4 *Ebook*

This book is dedicated to Kobe Bryant, his daughter Gianna and the seven other passengers who tragically lost their lives January 26th, 2020. Thank you Kobe for showing kids around the world what it means to leave a legacy and make an impact beyond the game.

CONTENTS

INTRODUCTION

Building my personal brand was something that I never thought about during my athletic career. Honestly, I don't even think I knew what a personal brand was when I was competitively playing basketball, let alone think I had one of my own. I quickly found out that the joke was on me as I began to make the transition into life after sports. It turns out this idea of having or developing a "personal brand" was something that was already being done for me without me even knowing it. It was something that was evolving and growing on its own, even though the only thing that I had ever focused on was becoming a better basketball player. It also turns out that every single athlete (yes you too) on this planet has one and if they aren't controlling it, then something or someone else is. It became more clear to me that if athletes don't control their own narrative and story, other people or the media will control it for them, dictating the perception that people have of that athlete. That can be a scary thing to think about, right? But it's the truth. And moreover, it's something I wish I had realized earlier in my playing career. Plus, I know for a fact that I'm not the only athlete who has said something like this before.

When I look back at the end of my athletic career, taking control of my personal brand was by far the most important thing that helped me transition effectively into life after sports, because it allowed me to see who I was outside of being an athlete, while also allowing other people to get to know my story as well. Over the past several years, I've watched so many of my former teammates and other athletes struggle to transition into life after sports. Many of them seemed like they were more than equipped and intelligent enough to make the transition, but when it came to disassociating themselves from being an athlete, they just couldn't seem to get past it. Being an athlete was all they knew. They had only tapped into the athlete side of who they were, never acknowledging the entire individual. They had no idea what else they could bring to the table or offer to the world. Without the ball in their hands—they essentially felt like a nobody.

But when you begin to take command of your personal brand, it forces you to figure this out. Crafting your personal brand helps you to establish a stronger identity of who you are deep down inside. It propels you to focus not only on what you can do or offer to the world, but also why you're the athlete or individual who can offer it. It's one of the only times when I can put a guarantee behind the saying, *"If you build it, they will come."*

Building a personal brand as an athlete still includes considering your athletic side, don't get it twisted. But believe me when I say that it's also a lot more than that. Building your personal brand gives you the ability to dive into your other interests, capabilities, and passions even if you're not sure what they are yet. It forces you to think outside of your physical capacity and discover the potential you have outside of the game you play.

It also shows people that you're not one-dimensional and releases you from the box that so many people try to put athletes in. Building a personal brand is about inserting yourself into the conversation in your own unique way and telling your story in the way you want to tell it. It shows that you are capable of so much more and that you are more than just an athlete.

What happens when athletes really take the time to build a brand for themselves?

1. *They influence more.*

2. *They earn more.*

3. *They win more.*

With all this being said—you still might be wondering what the exact definition of a personal brand is. Well, to sum it all up, your personal brand is defined as "your reputation, or how people perceive you." It is how people react to you and the emotions they have when they think of your name. It is not only who you are and what your story is, but it is also about what you value, what you stand for, and the things that you firmly believe in. It's how you dress, the way you talk, and the way you interact with others. It is essentially everything that makes you, you. For every athlete out there, this means not only who you are on the playing field, but more importantly, off the playing field as well. A brand incorporates how people feel about you as an athlete, but also their impression of you as a person in society.

The term *personal brand* became mainstream in the late 90s when it was highlighted by Tom Peters in an article for *Fast Company* magazine. He starts out the article by writing:

> Regardless of age, regardless of position, regardless of the business we happen to be in, all of us need to understand the importance of branding. We are CEOs of our own companies: Me Inc. To be in business today, our most important job is to be head marketer for the brand called You.

Of course this concept of personal branding had been around long before this quote, especially for athletes and celebrities, but it's been amplified and put under a microscope in recent years due to social media, the emergence of digital marketing, and social advertising. It's what we call a buzzword in the marketing and branding world. If you think about some of the most notable athletes in the history of sports—companies have always leveraged the relevance of these athletes to push and promote their products.

Michael Jordan is probably the most illustrious athlete who has become a huge cultural symbol, both on and off the playing field. But even before Michael Jordan, there was a baseball player by the name of Babe Ruth, who is credited for endorsing underwear and chocolate candy during his baseball career with the New York Yankees during the 1930s and 40s. Michael Jordan, however, took celebrity and athlete marketing to another level. He generated millions of fans, followers, and dollars (even before social media) not only through his basketball talent, but also with his personality and charisma. He completely changed the game for athlete branding. At the height of his basketball prowess, everyone wanted to be "Like Mike" igniting a Nike slogan which is still impactful and recognizable today.

Through his sponsorship deals—mainly with McDonald's, Gatorade, and Nike—Michael Jordan, along with his agent David Falk, proved to everyone that an athlete's value is worth more than what we see on the court or field. Aligning himself with David Falk, who is the genius behind the "Air Jordan" name, Jordan was able to tie himself to big name brands and companies which naturally led consumers to be enticed by these brands.

As according to plan, consumers began to buy more from these companies solely because of this association. Buyers were not only seeing Jordan on the court, they now began to see him on TV commercials, billboards, and hear him through the radio. The emotional connection, respect, and admiration that people had with and for Michael Jordan, directly transferred to the brands that he endorsed, which elevated both his profile and turned major profits for these companies. As a result, the Jordan brand is a billion-dollar entity that still drives our culture today.

Since those days, things haven't changed too much, except that more athletes are now aware of the abundance of opportunity out there. For example, think about former NFL quarterback Tim Tebow's brand and how he has maintained relevance despite having had a very subpar NFL career. Winning the Heisman trophy in 2007, he obviously had a very successful career at the University of Florida, but his talent didn't seem to translate over to the NFL well. He was nowhere close to being a great quarterback on the pro level, but people absolutely fell in love with him and he built loyalty amongst his fans because of certain qualities he possessed, along with the story he told to people about himself. His signature kneel became a phenomenon known as "Tebowing," and he actually led the NFL in jersey sales at one point during his career.

He has since transitioned out of football, but has still had many opportunities for broadcasting and writing books due to name recognition and the power of his brand. This is a major shift that has only happened in the last fifteen years or so, and I believe that we're only at the beginning of it. Part of the reason I'm writing this book is to prove that you no longer have to be the best player on the team to build a quality brand as an athlete. The days of the Michael Jordans and Tom Bradys of the sports world taking up all of the endorsements, sponsorship opportunities, and market share are gone. In today's world, as long as you can capitalize on your relevance while you're playing, and build your platform strategically and emotionally, you can have unlimited success both in and out of your sport. For the athlete who does this, the sky is literally the limit.

But for a lot of athletes, figuring out what your brand is, the other things you want to pursue in life, and how to communicate all of this can be very challenging. I get it. It's a lot of work and that's the main reason why many athletes don't even know where to begin. At the same time, it's also very worth it in the long run. The main intention of this book is to help you figure out that starting point. In addition to that, it's also here to teach you how to reach any level of success you want in life after sports. It's a blueprint from another athlete's standpoint to educate and guide you through the nuances and beginning stages of brand building, and how you can leverage it for the rest of your life.

Building your brand is an invaluable practice and I want you to see everything that it can do for you over time when you do it the right way. And as a side note, this is not just a book for collegiate and professional athletes either. It's for coaches, managers, financial advisors, agents, sports professionals, and anyone who has a passion for helping athletes grow in and out of sports. As I said before, regardless of skill or ability, every athlete...in fact, **everyone** has a brand. It begins when we're born and lasts all the way up to when we leave this planet; throughout this book, I'll show you how to build it and use it to have success in your future.

So upon reading this, you'll have two choices: guide and cultivate your brand, or let it be defined on your behalf. The opportunity is 100 percent driven by you. When you choose to build your personal brand, you make a decision to be an active partner in shaping the direction of your life. No matter how long you last in your sport, this is about taking advantage of the even-level playing field we have in life (pun intended) and setting yourself up for whatever might come your way in the future. Let's get started.

CHAPTER 1

WHY ALL ATHLETES HAVE TO BUILD THEIR PERSONAL BRAND

When I look at modern-day professional athletes, athletes such as Joel Embiid, Juju Smith-Schuster, and Mike Trout, I no longer see young rising stars in the NBA, NFL, and MLB, respectively. I see creative and innovative individuals who understand who they are intrinsically. I see athletes who attract attention from millions of fans on a daily basis. I see media and cultural influencers who have an incredible amount of power over the current generation—maybe even more so than the leagues they play in. I see game changers who have the capacity to move the needle for other athletes and individuals in the future. Joel Embiid's comedic personality and wittiness accurately illustrates what his brand is about, and he maintains this nature on and off the basketball court. Juju Smith-Schuster is fun and entertaining as he constantly makes an effort to engage with the younger demographic that follows his every move on social media. Mike Trout might be more reserved than other athletes online, but throughout the years he has been an incredible role model and community leader outside of baseball.

Each one of these athletes has a very powerful and impressive following online and offline, but more importantly, it seems they have all taken the time to identify and build an authentic brand that echoes outside of their sport as much as it does in it. These athletes know that they are no longer just athletes. They know that they are more than just your typical role models. They are among the people that we place on the largest pedestal in the modern world.

Athletes like LeBron James and Colin Kaepernick have been able to use their platform to shed light on injustice and inspire millions through social causes, which we'll discuss in this book. Athletes like Dirk Nowitzki and Albert Pujols have transcended boundaries for international athletes who have ambitions of playing in the highest leagues in America. And athletes like Venus Williams and Kristi Yamaguchi have shown other young female athletes that they can win on the playing field, as well as in the boardroom as entrepreneurs.

From high school superstars to the last man on the bench on the worst NFL team, every single athlete is admired by someone, somewhere in the world and every athlete holds that responsibility. Every single athlete, regardless of the level they play on, has the power to influence and impact those that aspire to be them or be like them. This responsibility within itself should be reason enough for all athletes to capitalize on this moment that they have right in front of them.

First, let's get one thing straight: many people won't tell you this, but playing a sport is a privilege—it's not an obligation. Once you understand this, you can begin to see and take advantage of every opportunity that you have while you're in the game. You become conscious of the fact that you have an amazing chance to impact and inspire people's lives. You begin to notice that this is a window that will eventually close, and if you want to maximize it, it takes careful planning, good intention, and great execution. In my personal belief, the number one reason why all athletes have to build a sustainable brand is because in the end, when it is all said and done, it's essentially all you have left. If you don't build your brand, subconsciously you will be keeping yourself in the box that I mentioned earlier—confining you as an athlete and nothing else. If your personal brand equals your identity, and your identity has always been nothing but "athlete" for twenty-plus years of your life, then reconstructing that identity becomes almost impossible once you retire.

Let's take a step back and look at the reality for a second

here. I think most of us know and understand that becoming a professional athlete is a rarity in any sport. Less than 2 percent of all NCAA student-athletes go on to become professional athletes, and there are nearly half a million student-athletes each year. Even if you do make it to that level, the average career length for an NBA player is 4.8 years. NFL is 3.3 years, and MLB is 5.6 years. You still have a lot of life left once you're not an athlete any longer. In most cases, there will be very few people who want to be in your corner once you're finished. Unless you're a Hall of Fame type player, there will be few people who care about what you did in your athletic career. There will be very few people who will remember your stats or accolades or whether or not you started or came off the bench.

The only thing that matters is this: either leveraging your time during your career to create more opportunities for yourself, or making yourself valuable to others once you retire. All that other stuff won't get you in any door once you're done, because the sad truth is that people only care about you when you're actually playing. Most people won't value you for who you are or what you think. Most people will only value you for what you can do on the court, track, field, or ice. They'll value you only for what you can do physically.

I'll give you a prime example. You might remember the name Steve "The Franchise" Francis. But then again if you aren't a basketball fan, you might not. I was a huge Steve Francis fan growing up and actually lived in the same house he was raised in for a short period of time. Steve Francis was the second overall pick in the 1999 NBA draft. During his NBA career he was a three-time All-Star and also won NBA Rookie of the Year in 2000. In the early 2000s many people thought that he had a long, promising career ahead of him, but he quickly fizzled out of the league at the young age of thirty-two. Now, even though it's been years since he's been out the league, he still seems to struggle with navigating through life after sports. During his career he had so much going for him, and I'm sure he didn't expect to be out of the league so abruptly, but sometimes that's just how it works out. It's a testament to why you have to be prepared to do other things besides just being an athlete. The *Players' Tribune* did a feature article on him in 2018. In it he says:

> I went from selling drugs on the corners in DC to the NBA in four years...and now it's over? It's a wrap? At 32? I knew it was the end, and that's some really, really hard shit to swallow. I don't care who you are.

Steve Francis is just one of thousands and thousands of stories of athletes whose careers didn't go the way they expected. Or even if it did, they still struggled with the realities of walking away. At the age of thirty, you still have your entire life ahead of you, whether or not basketball or any other sport is in the picture. Granted Steve Francis played at a time when athletes didn't necessarily have as many opportunities as they do today, but now there's hardly any excuse you could make. There are entirely too many other options out there for athletes. And from what I've seen, many of them aren't getting in on them. I was always taught that when there's money right in front of you, never leave it on the table—figuratively speaking of course. But if you're not building your life after sports while you're still playing, that's exactly what you're doing.

Building your personal brand and not just your athletic brand will present you with opportunities outside of your sport that you never even knew existed. It will help you connect with other people and allow you to build trust and more relationships. Most of all, it will help you identify who you are deep down inside and help with your transition into life after sports. The athletes that I've seen who have a harder time transitioning into life after sports and figuring out what they want to do next, are the athletes who wait to start preparing. They are the athletes who don't take advantage of their network, their brand, and what's in front of them while they are still playing. They are the athletes who don't recognize the power behind using awareness and attention to make things happen and the ones who let it fall by the wayside during their athletic career. They are the athletes who waste their time and think that the sports lifestyle is reality, or that it lasts forever. The moment you retire from the sport you play is usually the day that the recognition or notoriety goes away. That's literally the first day when people start to forget who you are. That's the day that the accolades don't seem to matter anymore, the camaraderie fades away, and you become an athlete that just "once was." It is a harsh reality that every athlete has to face one day. But who you are at your core never changes and when you build a brand, that's what you're trying to keep intact. This is about sustainability. It's about longevity.

Being an athlete is a very short period of time in your life, relatively speaking, and it goes by extremely fast. Even if you are fortunate to play until you're forty years old, you still have a lot of years left to do other things and create another profession. As long as you're an athlete, you have relevancy. As long as you're an athlete, you receive a lot of attention. As long as you're an athlete, you have a strong platform, but how you leverage and use that platform is 100 percent up to you. People admire you and look up to you. People want to be like you. People want to be in your presence.

This world where users single-handedly govern the media they absorb is the greatest time to create a brand for yourself. It is also the easiest. We no longer live in a time where major outlets monopolize the market and are in charge of everything that is communicated to the masses. We live in a time where we create our own stories, shows, and projects, and present a perspective that is our own. Done with the right intentions, this can be life-changing for anyone who is willing to put in the work.

A FEW ATHLETES WHO DID PERSONAL BRANDING THE RIGHT WAY
ALEX RODRIGUEZ

A great example of an athlete who has been able to build a very strong brand outside of athletics is Alex Rodriguez. Rodriguez was at one point completely banned from the MLB for using performance-enhancing drugs, and people were skeptical about whether or not he could recover from this. While his baseball career took a major hit and he faced negative reactions for this situation, he still is remembered in the baseball world as a model citizen and a great teammate. His company, A-Rod Corp, which he originally started at the age of twenty-six out of fear of being unprepared for the future, has a wide business portfolio that includes everything from commercial real estate to eSports, with brand partners that include UFC Gyms in South Florida; TruFusion, a rising fitness initiative which marries yoga, Pilates, boot camp, barre, boxing, and cycling; Energy Fitness, a large chain of high-end fitness centers primarily located in Mexico City; and NRG eSports, a millennial-focused content network, providing exclusive, multi-platform programming for gamers.

He was also the host of CNBC's show *Back in the Game*, in which he helped former pro athletes get back on solid financial footing. He has been able to do what a lot of athletes have struggled with in the past. He learned from his mistakes, he reinvented himself and the public's opinion of him, and he has come out on top. He has built a brand that portrays him as a savvy businessman, community leader, and on-air personality. A-Rod's legacy as a CEO will probably now outweigh his time as a New York Yankee, and by learning from guys like Warren Buffett of Berkshire Hathaway, and JPMorgan Chase's CEO Jamie Dimon early on, he is on pace to build his own empire while also creating a long-lasting personal brand.

VENUS WILLIAMS AND SERENA WILLIAMS

Venus Williams is another excellent example of an athlete who understood the power of building their personal brand. I mentioned her earlier in this chapter and for a very good reason. She is the founder and CEO of her own clothing line called EleVen, and consistently has taken advantage of her spotlight by wearing her own apparel while dazzling the tennis world with her play on the court. While this fitness apparel brand has been making waves since its inception, it's not even Venus's only business. She also is the CEO of the design company, V Starr Interiors. Venus has not limited herself to just being an athlete, and believes that athletes are designed to conquer challenges, so applying the lessons of resilience will definitely benefit her businesses as they grow. She found what she loved to do outside of tennis and created a lifestyle around that.

At the same time, I would be doing an injustice if I didn't mention Venus's sister, Serena, who is not only known for what she does on the tennis court but also how she has turned herself into an amazing businesswoman. Both she and Venus own a stake in the Miami Dolphins football team and, furthermore, have opened a community center in their hometown of Compton, California, to support residents affected by gun violence. She has also built her brand outside of tennis through her endorsement deal with Nike, and her own clothing line called Aneres—a handbag and jewelry collection on the Home Shopping Network (HSN). Serena has also planted herself in the Silicon Valley tech space as a board member for the company SurveyMonkey. For these two sisters to overcome the challenges as African American women from Compton, California, to build the brands that they have built is truly remarkable. They have created platforms that will be cemented forever, while impacting other African American female athletes at the same time.

SHAQUILLE O'NEAL

Although he was once known for breaking backboards and winning championships with the Los Angeles Lakers, Shaq is now respected as a huge personality and multimillion-dollar brand off the court. Shaq's portfolio includes endorsements such as Zales, Muscle Milk, Dove, Nintendo, Macy's, JC Penney, Comcast, Monster speakers, NBA 2k, Gold Bond, Buick, Taco Bell, Nestlé Crunch, Icy Hot, Pepsi, Wheaties, Oreo, and Burger King, just to name a few. He is also the joint owner of 155 Five Guys burger restaurants, seventeen Auntie Anne's pretzel restaurants, 150 car washes, forty 24 Hour Fitness centers, a shopping center, a movie theater, and several Las Vegas nightclubs.

One of the most impressive things to note is that his business career has made him more money and given him more success since he's retired from the NBA. Most of this success is due to his persona, charisma, and character which he completely owns and uses in everything he does. Most people don't even know that Shaq is also an in-demand DJ. A lot of athletes have the intangibles that can make them very successful in the business world, but that doesn't necessarily mean that it always transfers over that easily.

Alex Rodriguez, Venus Williams, and Shaq are successful athlete-turned-entrepreneurs who have built excellent brands for many different reasons, but one of the most important is their willingness to learn and adapt, as well as their understanding of how to take advantage of their brand. It is also in their inclination to realize what makes them special and unique and how to use this to stand out amongst other athletes. These athletes in particular understand the core of their brands and what makes them valuable as individuals, not just athletes. A-Rod and Shaq haven't seemed to struggle at all as they have transitioned into life after sports, and I'm sure Venus won't either once she decides to hang it up for good, because they all took the necessary steps to set themselves up for success well beforehand.

The common denominator is that all of these people took advantage of the short window they had as athletes and never stopped learning and maturing. Controlling your own narrative is one of the most important things that anyone can do in life, and not just in athletics. It is one of the only things that you are in complete control of when it comes to your professional career and your life. It is how you intentionally separate yourself in a world where everyone can appear the same. As an athlete you have a chance to not only create something that lasts well beyond your sport, but to also influence other athletes to do the same. Creating and scaling your brand is not just about benefiting from sponsorships and endorsements while you're playing, but it is about laying the groundwork for anything else that you might want to do going forward.

Now that we've laid out why it's important for all athletes to build their personal brand—you might still be thinking, "Why do I need to be a role model for anyone else? Why do I have to tell everyone my story and business? Why can't I just play my sport and let my game be my brand?" The thing is, you can. I'm not here to force any athlete to do something that's not in their heart or something that they don't want to do. But if it's a question about whether or not you have to be a role model, I want you to keep reading to see what Karl Malone said in response to Charles Barkley saying he did not believe that athletes are role models. In 1993, Charles Barkley partnered with Nike to create the "I am not a role model" campaign. In the commercial he stated, "I am not a role model, I'm not paid to be a role model." Furthermore he said, "I am paid to wreak havoc on the basketball court... parents should be role models." In essence, he is correct. Athletes aren't necessarily paid to be upstanding citizens and role models for others. Athletes are just paid to play and win games, right? On the contrary, since you're in the spotlight, being a role model is exactly what comes with the territory whether you like it or not. Hall of Fame power forward Karl Malone responded to the campaign in a *Sports Illustrated* column later that year stating:

> Charles...I don't think it's your decision to make. We don't choose to be role models, we are chosen. Our only choice is whether to be a good role model or a bad one.

Being a role model and having a brand is not a choice anymore. It's merely about who's controlling the message behind it. Who's telling the story? Who is influencing the public's perception? You can avoid putting yourself out into the world, you can avoid interviews and press, you can even avoid social media altogether. But you can't complain or be upset at the consequences or the chances you may miss by making it a priority in your career. Your brand is going to be what carries you over and allows you to maximize anything else that you want to pursue during your career or after you're done playing, not your game. Your brand is going to allow you to utilize relationships and partnerships during your career, not your jump shot or ability to hit home runs. Your brand is going to allow people and fans to get to know you for who you are and allows people to relate to you on a deeper level, not your celebrations in the end zone.

People do things or buy things from people they know, like, and trust, and that starts with your character, personality, and how you are perceived by people. We live in a society that is predicated on attention. Attention has always been the name of the game. Before you can sell to anyone, raise money, or make an effective change in any way, you have to have people's attention first. They have to know you exist and they have to understand what you're bringing to their attention.

Josh Hoffman of The Institute for Athlete Branding and Marketing describes it perfectly as the Attention Economy. He says, "In the Attention Economy, athletes are all competing for a finite amount of fan attention, and it's a zero-sum game. If fans are paying attention to someone or something else, they can't pay attention to you (the athlete) at the same time. And, if they're not paying as much attention to the athlete, this athlete is not maximizing the worth and value of his or her athlete brand." Whatever you want to do, say, promote, elevate, change, impact, or put out into the world starts with your brand and how people relate to it. Don't wait until it's too late. Start building today. You'll be thankful you did.

"The attention of the end consumer is all that matters, and when you understand where it is...that's where you need to strike, create and spend against."

—GARY VAYNERCHUK (CEO OF VAYNERMEDIA)

CHAPTER 2

YOUR MESSAGING, YOUR STORY, AND YOUR VALUES

I once heard a quote that said, "Getting ahead in life isn't about what you know or even who you know, it's all about who wants to know you." The minute I heard this, I really took it to heart and knew that this couldn't be any closer to the truth. If you can get people to be consistently and genuinely interested in who you are, that is the key to influence and impact. That is how you become a trusted authority in any capacity and what it really means to affect people around you. The people who others wish to know, talk about, and aspire to be like are the people who usually provide the most value. In return that usually equals money, influence, and respect in various ways. So in order to achieve a lot of these perceived "successes" that most of us want in life, you have to be in a position to get people talking about you.

You have to have something that is worth listening to or be so captivating that people desperately want to stop and to pay attention to what you're doing.

Of course, this is always easier said than done though. Especially when it comes to doing something of substantial value. Most people either don't give others a good enough rationale as to why they should be interested in them, or they struggle with the insecurities pertaining to the idea of people wanting to listen to or know about them—the basis for the concept of imposter syndrome. Most of us have a lot of insecurities that we face. Most of us have things we wouldn't dare to share with the world. Reaching greatness usually involves the fear of failure or the fear of success, but we all have to realize that each one of our stories matters equally, especially if we can show people what they can learn from them. When you're trying to make an impact and leverage your brand, the first thing you have to ask yourself is: *why should anyone want to get to know me or my story?*

I understand firsthand that it can be very uncomfortable being vulnerable and talking about what you've experienced. It can be hard telling the world about your failures, things that you've struggled with, or even things that you're currently facing. What you have to understand is that it's through those things that we find power as individuals. This is exactly the thing that makes your brand powerful and recognizable. Through your story, your background, and your life people will consider you to be more relatable and human, just like them. Your story shows other people that if you made it through adversity and came out on top, then they can do it too. It gives hope when hope might not have been there before. Most of all, when you're completely transparent and you let your guard down, it allows people to connect to you emotionally and builds an undeniable trust.

It's not always easy to be true to who you are and what you stand for in spite of what people might say about you. But knowing who you are, what you believe in, and staying true to those facts will allow you to bring about sustainability that lasts for a lifetime. You can think of it as you becoming the author of your life, and the way that you write the narrative is by crafting your personal brand, day by day and interaction by interaction. Nowadays, everyone can see through inauthenticity and fluff. We're constantly exposed to bullshit so we crave and even respect the reality that hits us in the face. Even if it's harsh and brash. And even if it's hurtful at times. You have to be real before anything else and be able to tell your story in a way that gets people curious about you and what you've been through. It is about showing the sincerest version of who you are, but also adding your unique personality to the dialogue. If you aren't being yourself or speaking your truth, it will eventually catch up to you and hurt your brand long-term. Most people try to fabricate who they are because they don't want to offend anyone or turn people off. They fear that if they show who they truly are, everyone won't like them. The goal isn't to have everyone agree or like you and your brand. The goal is to have a select group of people who love you and can relate to your message and story.

"You can please some of the people all of the time, you can please all of the people some of the time, but you can't please all the people all of the time"

—POET JOHN LYDGATE AS MADE
FAMOUS BY ABRAHAM LINCOLN

If you can find who your "tribe" is and show them your truth, that will create a lasting connection between you and those who admire you. In the past, I've had several athletes ask me things such as, "Well, what do I do if I don't have a story?" or "What if no one can relate to my experiences?" My response is always, "Everyone has a story to tell, whether you think so or not. And the good thing for you is someone, even if it's only one person, needs to hear yours."

They might not have been through what you've been through or achieved what you've been able to achieve, but that doesn't mean that your story isn't meaningful to someone in the world. That doesn't mean that you can't make a difference in at least one individual's life. I realized this when I published my first book called *Lessons from the Game*. Before releasing that book, I was literally terrified to talk about all of the obstacles I went through in basketball and throughout my life. But over time, I began to understand that even though it was my story, it wasn't really about me. My story was about the other athletes who might go through similar things that I went through and how I could help them get through those things. It was about me giving back and inspiring the next generation of dream-chasers and achievers.

The minute that I took the focus off me and my insecurities, was the minute that I gave myself the ability to connect with others on a deeper level. That was the minute I started taking 100 percent control of my brand. And when I started to speak out, my truth reflected positively on everyone who listened. Being true to who I am and what I have been through as an athlete set me free from those insecurities, because I openly told others about them. There weren't any secrets to hide behind anymore because I gave the world my story, and through that I started to build a brand that people were interested in connecting with. You want your brand to conjure some kind of emotion—not indifference. When people feel indifferent about something they tend to forget about it. A forgettable brand is an irrelevant brand and irrelevant brands don't generate opportunities. A great brand that lasts forever unequivocally draws out a strong emotion in someone, whether that emotion is good or bad.

When you take a powerful stance on something or over-come insurmountable odds, or express who you really are in the purest sense, you'll do just that. Think about why sports are so powerful. It's because they bring that emotion out of us. We love cheering for our favorite teams whether they are winning or losing. We love talking trash about our opponents during intense rivalry games. Branding is just like sports in that aspect. It's about the emotional conviction.

But you have to know who your story is for and who you are specifically speaking to. You have to know your audience intensely and thoroughly. Think about what scares them. Think about what inspires them. Think about what they need to hear from you. The better you know these things— the more you can use your story to elicit these emotions from them. Your only goal is to make a specific group of people make a concrete choice about you and make them feel very strongly about that choice. This all starts with your story, how you differentiate yourself as an athlete, and how you position yourself, which we'll dive into further.

OTHER KEY QUESTIONS TO ASK YOURSELF

It wouldn't be smart to do any of this or scale your brand without having a plan in place or at least an idea of how to apply it so it works to your advantage. Many athletes try to market themselves without thinking about the big picture, or thinking strategically about how they want to be looked at outside of their athletic career. Would you show up to summer training camp without an extensive off-season conditioning and nutrition program? Would you go into a game without scouting your opponent and having a defensive strategy in place? I highly doubt it. So you should never try to build your brand without first planning on the positioning and direction of your brand. Patti Hubbard and Stephanie Martin, co-founders of the athlete branding company BFWD (otherwise known as BrandForward) collectively say:

In building a brand, we encourage athletes to think about both short and long-term goals and objectives. This helps them to think less transactionally in the short-term and work towards a vision for life after sports, and results in them feeling more prepared on both a personal and professional level.

In today's world, athletes have the opportunity to pursue both their athletic goals and their personal passions at the same time. We want athletes to understand that they are multidimensional and that their identity should not be tied to just one thing.

By exploring all of their gifts, they can develop a brand game plan that looks at all of their interests. We've found this type of approach gives athletes the confidence to pursue their other interests while still playing and can provide them with a softer landing after sports as they are already actively pursuing something they are equally passionate about.

Therefore, in order to start preparing early and laying the groundwork, you have to ask yourself challenging questions that you might not even want to think about at this point in your life. These are questions that might feel unimportant or insignificant at first. You might even think that these questions can wait until you retire, but the longer you wait to answer them the more that you will identify as an athlete and only an athlete. These questions are the basis for how you will position yourself as a personal brand.

Start crafting your brand and figuring out who you are by asking yourself these key questions:

- What do I love to do other than my sport? (Another way of asking this is, "What am I willing to struggle for other than my sport?")
- What else am I good at?
- What is it that gets me out of bed besides my sport?
- What problems in the world make me upset?
- What have I been through that other people learn from or relate to?
- If I could be known for anything besides my sport, what would I want to be known for?
- If I could do one thing every day besides my sport and not get paid to do it, what would it be?
- What does my perfect day look like without my sport?
- Who do I want to be a hero to? (Be specific, this is how to find your target audience.)

- What do they need from me?
- How do they need to hear from me?
- Why am I the person to deliver this message?
- What charities, companies, or products do I want to possibly launch in the future?
- What are my short-term and long-term goals?

Now, you don't have to have in-depth answers to all of these questions, but once you have the answers to some of them, or can at least provide some insight as to what your brand is about, then you can start crafting your personal brand statement—which is the cornerstone for how others will perceive you. There are several different ways that you can craft a personal brand statement, but at the end of the day, it is simply combining who you are with what you do (uniquely) in one sentence. It is how you show your audience how you can help them and why they should look toward you over anyone else.

Jeremy Darlow, who is a top brand consultant and the author of *Athletes Are Brands Too* and *Brands Win Championships*, does a great job breaking this concept down in his books.

Here is an example of how to come up with your brand statement according to him:

1. **The frame of reference:** the landscape in which you are comparing yourself.

2. **The point of differentiation:** your brand differentiator.

For example, a positioning statement for someone like Super Bowl-winning quarterback Russell Wilson might be broken down like this:

FRAME OF REFERENCE: The star quarterback...

POINT OF DIFFERENTIATION: ...who is a role model on and off the field.

Here are a few of my personal examples below:

- **Russell Westbrook:** Russell Westbrook is the NBA MVP who is also a fashion icon.
- **Malcolm Jenkins:** Malcolm Jenkins is a Super Bowl Champion and a political activist.
- **Bryce Harper:** Bryce Harper is the MLB's young flashy superstar.
- **Pk Subban:** Pk Subban is an African American hockey player who is also a major philanthropist.

Having a personal brand statement is how people get to know you as not only an athlete, but also what you're passionate about and want to be celebrated for outside of your sport. It's how you separate yourself from the flock, so to speak. Here are a few other questions to think about that might provide some insight for how you should go about doing this:

1. *How are you thought of in other people's minds?*

2. *What distinguishes you from the thousands of other athletes who also play your sport?*

3. *What do people come to expect from you outside of sports?*

4. *What do people ask you advice or help for?*

BE AUTHENTIC AND PERSONAL, BUT UNDERSTAND THE FINE LINE

I mentioned why authenticity is so huge at the beginning of this chapter, but I wanted to elaborate on how you can be authentic to who you are, while also being cautious about sharing too much or being too personal. You already know that if you aren't being true to yourself or if people see you as inauthentic, that can harm your personal brand forever. Keep in mind, however, there is such a thing as oversharing.

*"It takes 20 years to build a **reputation** and five minutes to ruin it. If you think about that, you'll do things differently."*

—WARREN BUFFETT

Pay attention to where you should draw the line. You should always give people your most authentic self whether that's online, in person, or anywhere in between. But never feel pressured to share everything. Your fans, the media, or other followers don't need to know about your personal issues, your health problems, or things concerning your family for example. Figure out what you're most comfortable with, but at the same time always think about whether something you're saying or putting out into the world could be insulting or inappropriate to someone. That's the last thing you want when you're trying to build a brand from the ground up, so always think before you do anything online, and offline as well.

Even though you don't have to disclose every single detail about your life and what you do in your personal time, there is a sense of vulnerability that is necessary to display if you want to build a relationship with your fans or attract people to you. Dior Ginyard, who currently is the senior player manager at the NFLPA (National Football League Players Association) says, "The biggest mistake I see is players feeling like they're obligated to be an advocate for something or do something they're not really passionate about. That ends up hurting athletes in the long run because the motivation and passion isn't there to keep it going and showing."

If you're real with your fans and other people, more often than not they will be real with you in return. If you do make a mistake, own up to it and admit when you're wrong. If you think something is wrong or feels wrong, then it probably is. Don't fake the funk. As an athlete, you are unfortunately held to a high standard. Don't take this lightly because if you do, it can have life changing consequences for you and your reputation.

WHAT QUALITIES AND TRAITS MAKE YOU DIFFERENT?

Many athletes choose the safe route because they're afraid of alienating themselves from prospective partners, fans, and opportunities. This is one of the worst things you can do when you're building a personal brand. When you are the same as any other athlete, why would anyone pay attention to you? They could be getting the same thing from someone else. Think about it this way, if two of the exact same things exist in the same space at the same time, one of them probably isn't needed. You have to separate yourself in some way. It doesn't have to be something crazy or off the wall. It can be simple, but unique. It can be minuscule in your eyes, but can make a monumental difference in the eyes of the public. Whether it's some kind of hairstyle, the clothes you wear, your accent, or some kind of quirky thing you do that can make you stand out from other athletes, you have to make a conscious effort to separate yourself in order to be something unique, not a commodity. Commodities can be found everywhere.

Think about how former NBA star Dennis Rodman become

a well-known brand with his hairstyle, his rebounding and defensive skills, as well as his off the court antics. Think about how Randy Moss become a brand through his elaborate one-handed catches, celebrations, and trash talk on the sidelines. People might have been critical of them, but they undoubtedly knew who they were. These guys knew what made them distinctive in the eyes of others and used every chance they had to expose their differences. We need more athletes who are going to be unapologetically themselves.

You might like anime and skateboarding, yet you're a black football player—something that is probably not seen too often. Embrace that. If you're a white basketball player and you like hip-hop and books about philosophy, express the hell out of yourself. If you're an Asian hockey player from New York who likes painting and drawing, don't be afraid to let people know! Most people see the world through a stereotypical lens. When you eliminate those barriers and get people to see outside of what they might have believed about you before, you're intrinsically doing your part to change the world in some capacity. You should never have to apologize or compromise for being who you are. You should only do that when you're not being who you are. Be yourself and the right people will gravitate toward you.

REMEMBERING YOUR VALUES

It's very important for you to figure out what you value and what you prioritize in your life. Do you value your family more than anything else? Are you all about community and giving back? Is traveling and experiencing different cultures a necessity for you? This will help you make critical decisions in and out of sports, as well as give you a blueprint for how you live your life everyday going forward. Values give you a baseline, although they can and more than likely will change over time. If you're a collegiate athlete, your values might fall in line with your team or university's values, which could include excellence, integrity, leadership, humility, passion, perseverance, unity, responsibility, or anything along these lines.

As you grow older and begin to establish your career outside of that, whether that's as a professional athlete or not, you will start to discover what values you want to uphold or get rid of. If you can identify and build on these values, then you'll have a solid foundation for the moves to make with your brand. You'll have a clearer understanding of which opportunities are right for you and which aren't right for you. Values are an important part of your brand because they help you make decisions when you might not know what to do otherwise. As individuals our values ultimately define us. They form the foundation of what we commit to. And since you have to live with yourself and what you believe in, your values should be one of the most consequential things in your life. Without them, you become someone who adopts other people's values. And if you're trying to build a brand, you can't let your identity depend on the identity of someone else.

CONSISTENCY IS KEY

When it comes to your overall message, the color schemes you utilize, what you wear, and even the way that you speak, all of it plays a part in your brand. The things you do, say, or express on a consistent basis will ultimately tell people what they should know and believe about your brand. This not only includes the things listed above, but it also goes for your social media profiles. Take into account your pictures and videos, the types of things that you post online, and the frequency in which you post them. Think about the flow and overall impression of your profile, even down to the faces that you make in your content. All of these factor into maintaining a consistent brand profile.

Look at it this way. Using the two examples below, which of them is easier to remember at first glance:

1. *AAAAAA*

2. S8B2734

This right here is the difference between having a consistent brand profile and a brand profile that is inconsistent. Consistency is easy to remember and keep up with while inconsistency confuses your audience and distracts them. Furthermore, being consistent ties in with trust and dependability, which are what all brands are founded on. If your audience can trust that you are who you say you are, and that you are going to be that way every single time, then they'll always be loyal to you. You might feel like some athletes or big-time celebrities don't necessarily adhere to this, but believe me when I say they are probably the exception. There are very few brands that can get away with that. You want to be predictable even if you think it's boring and even if you think you're being repetitive. Predictability gets a bad rap sometimes, but always remember that people will forever pay for what they can consistently count on.

ATHLETES WHO DAMAGED THEIR BRANDS

Do you remember the name Lance Armstrong? When you hear his name you probably think of him getting caught for taking performance-enhancing drugs, not him actually winning seven Tour de France titles. At one point in time, Lance Armstrong was one of the world's most famous athletes, but the trouble that he has been through has cost him his entire reputation and over $100 million. Plus he has been facing a string of lawsuits from the US government at the time of writing. What about Ray Rice? Rice, who said he knew his NFL career was over once it happened, was suspended indefinitely from the NFL when a video of him hitting his then-fiancé in an elevator was released to the public by TMZ. He has not been able to make a return to the NFL, but has tried to change the public's perception of him by speaking out on domestic violence and getting more involved in the community. Does the name Barry Bonds ring a positive perception bell? The home-run king became a crucial figure in the MLB steroids scandal in 2007. He ended up finishing his career that same year after confessing to a grand jury that he used performance-enhancing drugs unknowingly in 2004, but he was still found to have obstructed justice. As a result, he ended up serving one month under house arrest and now his name will forever be associated with this scandal.

All of these famous athletes were once at the pinnacle of their sport. They were adored by millions of people, but one wrong move has changed many people's opinion of them. When you're at this level, that's all it takes—just one mistake. Obviously, you never want your name to be synonymous with something that's negative. You never want one instance to define your brand and your future. Remember, that's all it takes.

Regardless of whether you're in high school, college, or a pro, it doesn't take away from the fact that you have to have solid morals and beliefs that you stand on. These should be the guiding principles for every decision that you make, both on and off the playing field. People will remember the things that you do wrong far more than they remember the things that you do right. As you move along in your athletic career, it is important to keep this in mind when making any decision.

ATHLETES WHO HAVE TURNED WRONGS INTO RIGHTS
MAGIC JOHNSON

Magic Johnson is an athlete that immediately comes to mind when I think about athletes who faced something negative and were able to handle it appropriately. In 1991, he openly admitted that he had contracted HIV due to having relations with multiple women, which played a part in him retiring that same year. He had also just recently married and had a son on the way. At the time, the idea of HIV and AIDS was associated with homosexuals and drug addicts, so many people didn't know what to do or how to react to this news. Despite this being the case, Magic Johnson publicly admitted his faults and accepted full responsibility.

It has now been a long time since that day he stood up in front of the entire country and had the courage to confess this, but I would argue that was the best thing he could have done. Since then, Magic and his wife Cookie Johnson have been very active as advocates of HIV awareness and have helped millions of people. He founded the Magic Johnson foundation "to develop programs and support community-based organizations that address the educational, health and social needs of ethnically diverse, urban communities."

He has also been very active in developing urban communities as well as revamping his brand into that of an astute businessman. Although it seemed like Magic had taken a major loss, he has now completely changed the way people think about that situation.

TIGER WOODS

What about Tiger Woods? I'm sure one of the first things that comes to mind is his infidelity and marital transgressions, coupled with his run-ins with the law. In 2009, after numerous women came forward stating that they had affairs with Tiger Woods, he publicly admitted his "transgressions" and apologized to "all of those who supported him." Over the next several months he ended up losing numerous sponsorship deals, which resulted in billions of lost dollars, and he took an indefinite break from the game of golf. Tiger was also arrested in 2017 for a DUI incident in which he had five drugs in his system. He has since been admitted to rehab and has even made his return to the game of golf, winning the Masters in 2019—his most recent title win since the incident. Though his brand has not fully recovered, and will take a lot of time to do so, he is working toward a better future while earning back the trust of his fan base.

MICHAEL VICK

Michael Vick is known as one of the most athletic NFL quarterbacks of all time. Sadly, at one point in time, he was more remembered for what he did off the football field than on it. Although he has made amends and rectified the situation (in some people's opinion) when most hear Michael Vick's name, they usually think about his role in the dog fighting scandal. He served eighteen months in prison for that. Once he got out, he had an opportunity to come back and play in the NFL, but his career was never the same and he has since retired from the game. The past several years since his release from prison, he has attempted to rebrand himself and even held the position as the offensive coordinator for the Atlanta Legends football team of the Alliance of American Football. He has also held up his commitment to speak out against dog fighting—traveling around the country speaking to youth at schools, recreation centers, churches, jails, and prisons.

There are plenty of examples of athletes who have made one wrong move that cost them their money, attention, and entire career. Some have redeemed themselves, but most of them couldn't. For the most part, you can say that all of these athletes failed in at least one aspect of building the groundwork for their brand. Some of them didn't uphold their values. Some of them failed to be authentic in every sense of the word. Some of them just never got clear on who they were outside of being an athlete and what their story was about. If you fail to plan, then you plan to fail. Your brand is way too important not to take it seriously. Do the hard work upfront. Uphold your values. Be true to yourself and your fans. And lastly, never compromise your reputation by making one bad decision.

CHAPTER 3

FOLLOWERS + ENGAGEMENT = EVERYTHING YOU NEED

When you think about having a solid social media presence as an athlete, do you believe that it is more about the number of followers and fans you have, or is it about the actual engagement that you have with those fans and followers? While that is somewhat of a trick question, the truth is that it's not about one more than the other. It's about having both and knowing that they matter equally.

You might look at any athlete's social media profile and see that they have thousands and thousands of followers, but very low engagement, likes, comments, or interaction. Yes, their follower count might be impressive, and brands and people alike take notice of this, but if you aren't creating conversation or building a community with these people that follow you, then your follower count is almost null and void. I asked former New Orleans Saints wide receiver Brandon Coleman what his biggest regret was when it came to building his overall personal brand and he said:

> I wish I was more aware of the actual power of social media and how your profiles are viewed as resumes now, which can go a long way with you getting an endorsement deal, just for example.

That is to say, if you aren't taking full advantage of all of your social platforms, you're easily leaving future opportunities out of the deck. I want you to imagine this: You're walking down the street and you see [insert someone's name that you admire]. This is the moment you've been waiting for your entire life. This is the chance of a lifetime to walk right up to that person and let them know how much they inspire you and how much they motivate you. As you walk up to them and begin to speak, they walk right by you without saying a word, or even acknowledging you were there. They completely disregard you and act like you never existed.

When you don't engage with the followers that you have on social media, this is exactly what you're doing. Social media is supposed to be just what it says it is: social. It's about interaction, dialogue, and building relationships, not vanity metrics such as likes and heart-eyed emojis. The same thing goes for engagement on the other end of the spectrum. Even though you might have a lot of engagement, if you're an athlete with 500 followers on social media, the truth is nobody is taking you seriously. It's all about having a balance between the two. You want to have a very strong follower count, but you also want to make your fans feel like they know you intimately and on a deeper level. You want to make them feel like they're a part of an exclusive group. Exclusivity is always a win-win.

Now, for an athlete who has a ton of followers but doesn't have the time to respond to everyone, I can completely understand how challenging it can be to manage your community. It's hard and it's demanding, but again it's absolutely worth it in the long run if you can try to respond to the best of your ability. Even if you just take five minutes out of your day to send a "Thank you!" or a quick emoji, that kind of stuff means the world to people who admire and look up to you.

The key is to be active and seen on social media to attract what you want from it. You can't just be on it because everyone else is doing it. You have to build a united community that engages with you and feels like a part of your journey. You don't want to have people who constantly question why they follow you in the first place. You have to be attentive to your supporters and let them know they matter. You can't continually keep them in the dark. People want to be part of something greater than themselves. They want to feel included and join something that matters on a bigger scale. That is a huge part of what makes us humans. We are born to connect and bond. When you have people following you and you interact with them, you are creating brand loyalty—which is a key piece to having a strong following.

BRAND LOYALTY

noun: **brand loyalty**
The tendency of some consumers to continue buying the same brand of goods rather than competing brands.

You want to create brand loyalty among your community because that is an everlasting connection that is invaluable. Brand loyalty is the trust that keeps a customer coming back time and time again. Why do you think brands like Apple, Amazon, and Coca-Cola have been some of the top companies in the world year after year? A lot of it has to do with the brand loyalty that they've built with their customers over the years. You choose to repeatedly purchase products from these companies because of the brand that they've built. It's because you trust them and you know you're going to get great products and/or great service every single time.

This isn't a coincidence, it's all calculated. This is the

same thing that you have to do when it comes to building an audience and a fan base. Your followers can choose to follow and pay attention to thousands of other athletes, but how can you make them loyal to your brand? How can you command their attention and get them to come back for more from **you**? This is the way you have to think because branding and marketing is a psychological game. On the surface, social media is just a combination of math and creative elements which is what makes posts, pictures, and videos successful or not. The athletes who understand how to garner attention and keep it are the ones who create that long-term brand loyalty. They are the athletes that maintain relevance and remain top of mind to consumers and brands. They are the athletes who will be able to generate money because they have earned it over other athletes. You have to decide how you're going to create your own top-notch brand loyalty.

ATHLETES WHO HAVE TOP-NOTCH BRAND LOYALTY

MARIA SHARAPOVA

Maria Sharapova and her father, Yuri, came to America when she was very young in hopes that she would become the tennis star she is today. By the age of fourteen she had turned pro and by the age of eighteen she was the world's highest-paid female athlete, which is a title that she held for eleven years. During this time, she had become a silver Olympic medalist and one of only ten women to win a career

Grand Slam in tennis. Her ability to perform on the tennis court combined with her stunning looks and attractive personality afforded her opportunities to expand her brand and partner with companies such as Canon, Porsche, Nike, Head, and Evian. To take it a step further, she established her own brands as a businesswoman creating Sugarpova, a global candy line.

The brand loyalty that fans have for Maria was really apparent in 2016 when she was banned from tennis after testing positive for meldonium, a heart medication that was on the list of prohibited substances at the beginning of that year. A few of her biggest sponsors, including Porsche and TAG Heuer, dropped her, while the United Nations suspended her status as a goodwill ambassador with its development program. With a following of over 27 million people across Instagram, Facebook, and Twitter, many people thought that her brand and businesses would back track and take a hit.

Instead, Maria and her team went headfirst toward that perceived setback and her brand never appeared to miss a step. Along with her team, she just put more time into learning about the business world, attending meetings, and even interning under Adam Silver, commissioner of the NBA, during the fifteen-month ban she faced. Fast forward to present day, her company Sugarpova does millions in sales across multiple countries. As you can see, the tennis legend's brand isn't going to slow down anytime soon due to the loyalty that her fans and followers have toward her in spite of adversity.

CRISTIANO RONALDO

When you think about some of the top soccer players in the world, Cristiano Ronaldo is pretty high on that list, if not number one. Originally from Portugal, Ronaldo signed his first pro contract with Manchester United when he was only eighteen years old. Fast forward to 2019, and he is one of the most paid and notable athletes in the world. At the time of writing, he has over 150 million followers on Instagram, 122 million on Facebook, and 75 million more on Twitter. He reportedly also charges upwards of $400,000 per sponsored post on social media solely because of his audience and engagement rates.

There are very few athletes that can command prices like that just for social media posts. He also has several endorsement deals which bring in millions of dollars each year including Nike, Herbalife, EA Sports, and American Tourister. Not included in this is his own company, CR7, and various branded products including shoes, underwear, fragrance, jeans, a children's line, a line of hotels, and soon-to-open restaurants in Brazil. Ronaldo has parlayed his success on the soccer field into multiple business opportunities outside of the sport. His millions of social media interactions and views per post have given him a platform that can be leveraged in a number of different ways.

Even when he was caught up in a tax evasion case with Spanish prosecutors, his brand never took a loss. No sponsors dropped off and his CR7 products still appear to be doing well. The strength of Ronaldo's brand and social presence continues to grow to this day and when it is all said and done, he will go down as one of the most influential athletes of all time.

YOUNG ATHLETES WHO ARE CHANGING THE GAME THROUGH SOCIAL ENGAGEMENT

ZION WILLIAMSON

I mean it's literally like he just came out of nowhere. At sixteen years old, Zion Williamson emerged into the public spotlight and was put on the world's platform as a 6'6", 270-pound "once in a generation" type player, with an athletic ability that hasn't been seen since LeBron James. In an era where anything and everything involving sports is broadcast on Instagram, Twitter, and Facebook, Zion became known for his physical nature, off the chart leaping ability, and inhuman-like highlight reels practically overnight.

Because of Instagram, Zion's brand was established well before he stepped onto Duke University's campus as a freshman in 2018. At the time, he had about 2 million followers on Instagram, putting him in a tier that included other young, rising NBA players such as Kyle Kuzma, Donovan Mitchell, and Jayson Tatum.

Can you imagine being eighteen years old, with 2 million people watching your every move? Two million people waiting to see what you're going to do next. Two million people praising and applauding you only for what you can do with a ball. It's a fascinating world that we live in to say the least, but for these young athletes who make it to this level, this is something that comes with the territory in the era of social media. Zion will have his every move observed by media, fans, and others, probably for the rest of his life. The pressure he will have to live under will be unfathomable. In some people's eyes, he is already regarded as the greatest high school basketball player of all time.

Although this statement might be debatable, you can't deny the truth that he is, without question, the most notable high school athlete of the social media era. This means his following isn't going anywhere anytime soon. And as he embarks on his NBA career, there will be plenty of other people who will be knocking at his door, whether it be for endorsements, sponsorships, partnerships, or any other deal that'll get him and them paid. The sky is the limit for young Zion because not only does he have a massive following that continues to grow by the day, he has the personality and character to back it up. Zion might be the exception as far as athletic ability goes, but let's look at some other young athletes who are also making a name for themselves through social content.

JAYLEN HUFF AND MAXWELL "BUNCHIE" YOUNG

These names might not ring a bell on the national level yet, but believe me when I say that they will soon. Jaylen Huff and Maxwell Young are two young football phenoms who both have social media followings that have exploded because of their talent on the field. They each have over 50,000 followers respectively and multiple scholarship offers to several different universities. As I'm writing this, they're not even in high school yet. Both of their profiles feature insane workout videos and viral football highlight clips that have been consumed by millions of people. If you were to take one look at their Instagram pages, you would immediately see that football is not just a sport for them. It's a lifestyle. They live and breathe it. It's not just a game. It's their destiny.

Becoming viral sensations through social media has given them opportunities to mix with many of today's professional athletes. They've graced the covers of magazines, they've been featured by major media outlets and news channels, and they've even done campaigns with global brands such as Under Armour. Their platforms have also given them the chance to be role models and examples for other young athletes who hope to pursue their dreams. Being that young and having that kind of attention is very difficult, so it's impressive how they seem to have been able to handle it so maturely. What we all have to realize is that marketing and promotion has become as much of every sport as actually training and playing.

Bunchie and Jaylen's parents are clearly well aware of this and have jumped at the opportunity to use their children's God-given abilities as a means to do big things. Some might consider it to be irresponsible or unethical for them to put their kids in the public's eye at such a young age. I say that this is the world that we're headed toward anyway; and furthermore, the numbers don't lie. These aren't the only young athletes who have gained this type of attention on social media and there are plenty of other young mainstream athletes who are reaping the benefits—so why not get in on the game? If any young athlete wants to get to the next level and actually stand out, their personal brand has to become as much of the equation as being good in the sport is. No eyeballs equals no exposure. And no exposure equals no opportunities to reach the next level.

SIMONE BILES

Simone Biles burst on the scene as a gymnast almost as quickly as Zion Williamson did. In 2013, at the age of sixteen, she became the first female African American athlete to win gold in the all-around US P&G Championships. Immediately, Simone became a national celebrity. While most kids her age were getting ready for the school week, Simone was being interviewed and observed by some of the top journalists and reporters in the country.

Over the years, Simone has appeared to handle her success well. With over 3 million followers on Instagram, she's an incredible inspiration for future gymnasts as well as young women all over the world. With this strong platform, Simone has attracted numerous endorsement deals over the years such as Procter & Gamble's Tide, United Airlines, Hershey's, Core Power and GK Elite Gymnastics, and Kellogg's. She's dominated her sport of gymnastics, created a brand that inspires others to work hard at their passion, and consistently displays power, confidence, and personality, despite her four-foot, eight-inch stature.

What I really like about Simone's social media platforms is that she posts several times a day, almost every day, which is a big reason why her brand and following has continued to grow (remember consistency). Even though gymnastics is not a top sport in the US and she doesn't even compete year-round, she's been able to constantly provide value to her audience and to the brands that she works with regularly.

But being a superstar athlete at a young age comes at a price. These kids often have to give up a lot of the things that their friends have. They don't have what we know as normal childhoods because they put so much into becoming a prolific athlete. And because they have these large followings online and in real life, they have to carry the heavy responsibility of staying clean 24/7. This could be you right now as you're reading this. You could have thousands of fans on social media and struggle with filtering out the negative comments, trolls, and critics. It's a lot to deal with, and can be extremely taxing, but learning how to manage it with levelheadedness and sensibility can put you in an echelon of your own.

The cost of brand success and popularity is crazy at times, but the trade-off can be life changing. Your platform as an athlete can be the leverage that gives you clout forever— not just during your athletic career. Of course not every athlete will have the bandwidth or talent to do this, but having just a small percentage of people who are loyal can create monetary success in the future. Exposure is happening at younger and younger ages. Kids are now well aware of what a brand is and what authenticity looks like online.

The digital age has given us a close up look at everyone's life, which consequently puts more pressure on young, talented athletes to succeed. It's becoming that much more important for young athletes to conduct themselves appropriately online. Social media is a tool and when you know how to use it the right way, the opportunities can be limitless. With that being said, let's dive in...

CHAPTER 4

HOW TO USE AND LEVERAGE SOCIAL MEDIA PLATFORMS

Social media has clearly altered the way we interact and the way we communicate with one another. It has changed the way we buy products, use services, and how we relate to our favorite brands, celebrities, and entertainers. Furthermore it has changed how we tell stories, generate ideas, and promote creativity.

In my opinion, the power of the internet and the applications that we use on a daily basis are still highly undervalued and underestimated. In 2006, as I was entering high school, social media barely existed—which tells me that we are only at the beginning of this new wave of technology. The internet is what the world now focuses on, and where people's attention is fixed. It is where we spend almost all of our time and it consumes a ton of our energy every day, largely without us even realizing it.

Having the ability to control and distribute your content is incredibly important in a world where most adult consumers spend more than eleven hours per day watching, reading, listening to, or simply interacting with some form of media. Knowing that this is where the world will continue to be for years to come, as an athlete it is the prime time for you to take advantage. From Instagram to YouTube, while these platforms might change names and evolve over time, the focus on the internet will not.

"When it comes to laying the foundation for your brand, it all starts with what you want to be known for, and then wrapping a story around those values. Concrete visuals (social media) help because they enable people to connect and identify with your brand."

—STEPHANIE MARTIN (FOUNDER OF BFWD)

It might seem like there are so many bad things happening in the world, but if you take a closer look you'll see that we are really living in an incredible time of innovation and impact. From time to time people will try to talk about the negative side effects and adverse consequences of social media, but I believe it's more important to think about how we use the platforms. We can't ignore the way that social media has made the world a better place, whether through social causes and raising money, or bringing awareness to certain events and celebrating individual accomplishments. People have been able to utilize the internet to literally change and save lives. We can't disregard that it's brought people from all over the world together, creating lifelong relationships between people who wouldn't have ever known each other otherwise.

Social media has become the norm for everyone—from kids in elementary all the way to elderly people in nursing homes. The medium has become more readily accessible over time, as the world transforms faster than we have ever seen before. It is extremely important for people to grasp this truth, especially when it comes to doing business and building sustainable brands. In the same vein, celebrities, influencers, and athletes (old and new) have to understand how critical this is to their future.

Keep in mind that as humans, we only consume stories or content in three simple ways: through reading text, watching videos, or listening to audio. These are the ways we get the information and entertainment we want. The way in which we consume text, audio, and video might change, but these methods of communication will more than likely never change.

While social media and the internet are beneficial in many ways, at the same time, the amount that we rely on and consume it causes attention spans to become shorter by the day. This means that staying relevant as a brand or an athlete is becoming harder by the day as well. If you want to stay above the noise and get the most out of social media, then posting frequently will certainly put you in a better position than your athlete counterparts.

One of the biggest reasons why athletes, or anyone else for the matter, struggle with building their brand on social media is because they are overcome with the fear of curating "perfect content," or they are too concerned with trying to post something that is going to get them likes instead of simply providing something that is valuable for their audience. Instead of being worried about what other people think about your social media content, focus on giving value. What you have to understand is that you can't overwhelm yourself with trying to come up with perfect posts on any platform, because there is no such thing. Doing this will only leave you stagnant—eventually resulting in you not sharing your story with the world.

Number one reason why people don't create on social media... *"Fear of what people think."*

DOCUMENT VS. CREATE

As an athlete, you have something that a lot of people don't have when it comes to creating good content. You have the luxury of structure. Meaning that most of the time, you know what your day is going to look like. You know that you'll work out, or do something pertaining to your development as an athlete. If you're a student-athlete, you know when you'll go to class, study hall, meetings, etc. This allows you to document and post whatever you're doing daily on social media for your audience. Of course, having a strategy behind how you do this is important, but this structure frees you from feeling as if you have to be crafting or coming up with new content all the time. All you have to do is take people on the journey with you daily. Provide valuable information and educate your audience on what's happening or what you learn on any given day. Combine this with being your natural self and you can build something very special.

Personal Branding = Education + Entertainment

The main things to consider are how you can tell unique stories on each platform, who your audience is on each platform, and how to be as authentic as possible. All athletes have to realize that each social media network is different. There are subtle variations that you have to be aware of when you're posting.

Each social media site creates a different mindset when you consume content or interact on them. It's the same thing we do in real life. The way you might act around your parents is different from how you act with your closest friends. The way someone interacts and engages on Twitter or Instagram is going to be very different from how someone interacts and engages on LinkedIn. This is exactly why a picture or video might gain more traction or engagement on Twitter than it does on LinkedIn and vice versa.

Acting one way on Instagram and acting differently on LinkedIn is not about you being fake or disingenuous. It's just contextual. Since we don't act the same way on each outlet, context always has to be taken into consideration when putting out content on each relevant outlet. At the end of the day, we are all essentially competing for the end user's attention. We want people to be invested in us and what we have to say or sell. The way in which you market and tell stories on these outlets has become key because everyone has a voice and opinion. You could have the best product or service or message but if no one knows about it, how will it ever sell or be noticed? If you don't have a connection or relationship with your audience, why would they buy from you? It goes across the board for businesses or personal brands. You have to have a deep understanding of how to operate on each platform and how people interact on them to gain attention for your brand. Below I've broken down some of the major platforms and specific ways to use each one to amplify and grow your own brand.

TWITTER

We've all heard the stories of professional athletes who tweeted something that was worded improperly, misinterpreted by the public, or simply taken out of context. We've seen the consequences and how they can perpetuate the narrative behind an athlete's brand forever, or at least change the way people think about them for a very long time. There can be a lot of negative outcomes for athletes who speak freely on Twitter, taking advantage of their First Amendment right, even though that's what they should be allowed to do. But since people don't often give athletes the same leeway as people in other professions, there's a thin line between what they could say and what they should say.

Looking from the outside now, I recognize how this can be both good and bad, as it comes with a lot of responsibility and requires maturity. Any intelligent athlete who realizes this also sees the great opportunity that lies ahead of them, especially if we're talking about a platform like Twitter. In 2016, *Forbes* released an article titled "50 of the Best Athletes on Twitter in 2016." Though this article came out several years ago, some of these athletes include LeBron James, The Rock, and John Cena, all of whom have built brands that are relevant and prominent both in and out of their respective sport.

They also happen to be some of the wealthiest former or current athletes in this day and age. It begs the question, is there a direct correlation between an athlete's financial success and their activity/engagement on social media? I believe there is to a certain extent. It's usually the athletes who interact with their followers in a genuine way who attract the most endorsements, sponsorships, and various streams of revenue. Winning and being good at your sport matters, but ultimately brands and big-name companies are all about eyes, awareness, and attention.

At one point, many people thought Twitter was a dying social platform. Somehow it has withstood the test of time and is still one of the most optimal media outlets for athletes to get their messages across, tell their stories, and build their brand. In March of 2018, Kevin Love posted an article on the *Players Tribune* which highlighted his battle with mental health issues and panic attacks. While he received overwhelming support and admiration for the article, it was this tweet which received over 7,000 retweets, 64,000 likes, and plenty of other direct replies in a matter of hours:

> Wow...I can't even describe how grateful I am for the love and support. More than anything, it's been amazing to see YOU tell your own stories about Mental Health. Let's keep it going. If want to share your story you can email me at kevin@playerstribune.com (yes, I'll read it)

By taking this powerful stance in talking about his struggles, he exponentially grew his influence, brand, and relevance in a matter of days, primarily due to his reach on Twitter. Through this one tweet, people fell in love with Kevin Love the person—not just Kevin Love the athlete. I'm sure that he stills receives tons of replies, comments, and emails because of this tweet and article. Because of his authenticity and transparency, people now see Kevin Love in a different light. They feel like they can relate to him and better understand that athletes experience the same things as other people. What Kevin Love did took an extreme amount of courage and guts, but ultimately it helped make him more "human" and genuine to his fans, which is a huge part of building a successful personal brand.

Moreover, because Kevin Love leveraged the power of social media, he elevated people's perception of him. He also created more awareness around mental health problems not only in the NBA, but around the world. He has given other people the courage to tell their stories as well. People now look to him as a hero who has given a bigger voice to those people who experience mental health trauma. Twitter is still powerful for this reason alone.

Kevin's story illustrates that you can create an immense reach on Twitter if you are honest and real with your fans. What is even more amazing is that Kevin took the time to respond and interact with others who have been through similar things. Not many athletes would take the time to read and respond to other people's stories and actually care, but he did. It isn't always about talking and sharing. When you're an athlete, especially a popular one, sometimes it's way more meaningful to sit back, observe, and listen to people. It means more than you'll ever know when you actually take the time to pay attention to people on Twitter. Half of your time should be spent engaging with other people and responding thoughtfully to any positive replies you get.

Most people don't listen—most people talk. We have enough people talking—we need more listeners. We need more people creating and responding to unique perspectives and conversations. We need more people who are going to do the things other people aren't willing to do because that's how you stand out amongst the rest. If you learn one thing from the Kevin Love example let it be this: speak your truth, but when it is time to listen to others, listen.

Building a brand on Twitter doesn't happen by trying to overpower the noise, and once you start to build your following and fan base, you have to continue to leverage interaction through thoughtfulness. You can't just post a tweet here and there and hope things happen for you. Everything takes longer than you think, and building a quality personal brand as an athlete happens with one person at a time, through one interaction at a time, with one reply or one emoji at a time. You have to constantly engage and talk to your followers like they're people walking past you on the street. You have to give them time to trust you and get to know you. If you do this, people will want to follow you and want to know what you're up to, regardless of whether you play in another game or not.

It's all about using Twitter to build trust and quality relationships that last during your athletic career and through anything else that you want to do in life. You never know where one interaction might lead. You never know who knows who and what can happen if you build the right relationship with the right fan. Treat everyone the same and never think you're too good to converse with someone. Trust me, all of this matters and if you want to have options for the future, you'll start going about this the right way. No matter what people say about Twitter, it still holds power and it will continue to hold power in the future because it is the only true social platform where personal human engagement and true interaction drives the core of the platform.

FACEBOOK

Facebook is one of the oldest social media platforms that still holds some weight in our culture today. Similar to Twitter, there have been speculations that Facebook is also on the decline, but that couldn't be further from the truth. With over 2 billion users on the platform, most people don't realize that Facebook has the largest user base of any social media platform. And even as Facebook has faced much scrutiny and criticism due to privacy issues and leaked data, it hasn't seemed to have a major negative impact on people using the platform.

Most people use Facebook just to check updates from their friends and family, post an occasional picture or video, and send and receive messages with the people they're closest to. As an athlete trying to build and scale a powerful personal brand, you need more capabilities and options than just those basics. Facebook has a lot of tools that can be utilized to grow a powerful brand and reach a wider demographic. This is exactly why any athlete who is trying to build a strong personal brand has to create and use a fan page rather than just a regular "Facebook Profile." The Facebook fan page, though it has decreased in reachability since its inception, was created for businesses or brands who want to connect with more people and tell them in detail about their product or service.

Your Facebook profile simply won't give you the same abilities and extensions as a fan page. Your profile won't allow you to connect with as many people as you need. A regular profile and a fan page are two totally different concepts. The number one reason why you want to use a fan page is to scale and expand the way you share your story. You want to show as many people as you can who you are, what you're about, and why they should follow your brand. When it comes to building a sustainable brand, the idea is no different from using any other platform. You want to build a deep connection with your audience and reach as many people as possible. Here are a few other reasons why you should start using a Facebook fan page for your athletic career rather than just using your regular profile:

- **You can create a larger base of followers.** It's a lot easier to make connections and interact with your fans with a fan page, which makes it more manageable to leverage your following on Facebook to gain partnership and sponsorship opportunities.
- **Sharing your journey becomes more seamless.** It is a fast and easy way to share your own story, as well as any other people's content if you want. If you're the type of athlete who doesn't mind the extra attention, you can take people behind the scenes and give them an inside look into your day-to-day life. (Host Q&As, fan giveaways, contests, etc.)
- **A Facebook fan page is more professional than a personal profile.** Imagine having your fans contact and connect with you through a personal profile. It is less professional and credible, especially as your community grows.
- **You can measure and track clicks, likes, visitors, and other data and analytics to know what type of content your fans like.** This information will be important for knowing what your fans want to see and what they

don't want to see as you post more content going forward. Imagine how fast you can grow if you can know what your audience likes beforehand.

A bonus is that you are able to integrate it with Instagram and run different ads on both platforms to increase engagement, noticeability, and even product/merchandise sales when the time is right. I know you've seen sponsored posts by other influencers and celebrities. Depending on how strong your brand is, you might not have to use ads, but if you do, a fan page is ideal for linking your ads to Instagram and targeting certain demographics.

Statistically, Facebook is still keeping up as one of the most relative platforms to use because of the number of users it has. Having a Facebook fan page gives you the chance to reach millions of people worldwide in a way that your regular profile can't. This is not to say that a personal Facebook profile isn't useful to have, but it definitely has its limitations.

INSTAGRAM

Depending on what your social media goals are, who you're trying to reach, and the message that you are trying to get across, different social media platforms will be more beneficial for you than others. And as we're going through this, I understand that it can be overwhelming to try to figure out which ones will make the most impact on your brand.

Instagram is absolutely one of those platforms that will be beneficial no matter what. Now, Instagram might already be at the forefront of your social media strategy and something that you use on the daily, but let's dive into why you need to be making use of it in the correct way to build your brand. More and more brands are investing dollars into ads, influencers, and marketing on Instagram because they recognize the potential and growth in the future. It has a user base of over 1 billion people and is currently growing rapidly year by year. With these stats, Instagram is currently the second most popular social media platform in the world behind Facebook, which actually owns Instagram. But to really get into the nuts and bolts of why it is so crucial for athletes to build and grow their Instagram page, you have to first understand a little about psychology and human nature.

Intrinsically, humans are very visual. We process visual images and content 60,000 times faster than we process text. If you think about it, everything in the sports world is about that as well. With video on the rise as a medium, Instagram has built their entire platform around this idea. We love to consume photos and videos. This is by far the number one form of social media for this type of consumption. Because Instagram is a very image intensive platform, it allows athletes the ability to showcase and share so much with their fans and followers. Everything from their workout routines, to meal plans, action shots, treatments, and everyday life can be displayed on Instagram in unique and creative ways. It's somewhat of a combination of multiple different social media applications in the way that it allows the user to post pictures and videos, along with long text descriptions.

Instagram is also very simple to understand and easy to use, along with an aesthetically pleasing layout. Plus, the demographic on Instagram is very diverse, therefore you can reach the exact audience or market that you want to reach without any problems. Whether you're a student-athlete or a professional athlete, you're always on the go and rarely have a day that doesn't include some type of activity. A lot of influencers and celebrities host two-way Instagram live feeds where they do contests and giveaways in which the winner can receive a prize, like a ten-minute call or meet up with them, for example.

You can even post an IG TV video of up to an hour of your workout and allow fans to see how you get better every day. There are endless ideas that you can implement with Instagram that helps build awareness and recognition around your personality, who you are, and what you're up to. These tactics are crucial in terms of building a relationship and rapport with those who support you and follow your every move. They want to know more about you and you can give them that access to create a lifelong bond. Think about what others are doing on Instagram and then think about what you could do differently that makes you stand out from the pack. There is really no "one size fits all" social media strategy for athletes, but every athlete should be taking advantage of it.

One of the most important things you can do for your future and your career is to invest in your fans and followers through Instagram. Document, don't just create. Understand your audience and what they want to learn and hear from you. Most importantly, engage with them as much as you can. Take a second and think back to how it felt when you were a kid and you went to your first professional or college sports game. Then think about whether or not you got the chance to meet, shake hands with, or get an autograph from your favorite athlete or any of the players on either team. If you did, how did you react? What was that feeling like? Now, think about kids in this digital era and how life-changing it would be if you responded to them on Instagram.

This is why it is important to say, "Thank you for your support" or even just giving them a thumbs-up emoji. People want to feel special and appreciated. On social media, and in particular Instagram, you have a great opportunity to do that for someone and it costs you nothing but a little time out of your day. You never know when you have an opportunity to change someone's life or when someone might change yours, and Instagram is the perfect place for this type of interaction to take place.

LINKEDIN

When you think about athletes on social media, LinkedIn is the last place you'd think they'd be. But in reality, LinkedIn is one of the best places for any athlete looking to expand their brand and find professional or business opportunities.

Whenever I come across the profiles of athletes on LinkedIn, many times I notice they are going about it all wrong. They either have a bland and incomplete profile or they don't tailor their message and bio toward what they are trying to accomplish. Everyone already knows what team you play for and when you were drafted. Everyone can google your stats and see the things you've done on the court or field. I've seen numerous athletes put this type of information on their LinkedIn page despite the fact that this isn't necessarily the place to display this kind of stuff.

Instead, athletes should be talking about their goals and aspirations for life after sports and what other career interests or passions they have. They should be using every section of their page to highlight their hobbies, other involvements, and ideas for what they want to be doing once their athletic career is over. Furthermore, they should be taking advantage of every chance they have to make an impression on people who come across their profile, whether that person is a fan or not (your profile could turn them into one). You have to realize the full potential of LinkedIn for your long-term career goals and transition process. With more than 500 million users, LinkedIn is sure to be the central hub for professional development in the future. LinkedIn is a foundational aspect of reaching long-term career success for athletes.

Start creating content showcasing that you're more than an athlete and ensure that it resonates on LinkedIn. You know that you're not just an athlete, but everyone else needs proof of this. The truth is that no one wants to hear about how many touchdowns you scored or points you dropped in your last game. This platform is strictly about business opportunities. Being an athlete can get you in the door, but what's going to keep you there? LinkedIn is the perfect platform to start showing people you have a sincere enthusiasm for developing professionally.

Do you want to start your own charity? Do you want to start investing? Do you simply want to find a job for when you're done playing? With the ability to write in-depth articles and put out images and videos that align with industries and business sectors that you might be interested in, you can show that you're multidimensional. Athletes should also be joining different groups and participating in conversations that fall in line with their career interests. They have groups for everything from life coaching and training to digital marketing and real estate. Showing and telling other people that you want to do and be other things besides an athlete opens the door for collaboration and opportunity.

Within your profile, you don't necessarily have to create a high volume of content, even though it would help you drastically, but you do need to be consistent and sincere at all times. Always be thinking in a professional mindset when exchanging dialogue on LinkedIn. That is the number one difference between LinkedIn and all of the other platforms. You should also constantly update your profile as you update your career.

As you go further along into your athletic career, things will change personally and professionally. If you're a student-athlete, you might do volunteer work or take a class that allows you to gain a new skill. If you're a professional athlete, you might get traded, released, or picked up by different teams. You also might join or partner with a company or participate in an externship. You might even venture out to do some public speaking in the community—something you could highlight on your page. If you develop a new skill such as public speaking, put that down and look for people to endorse you. If you start writing for a publication or happen to be featured on a major media outlet, add that to the appropriate section and provide some context with it. It is so important to stay relevant and show people that you are actually taking action offline, not just talking about it.

Whatever the case might be, your page has to reflect your career moves on and off the playing field and you need to constantly update the information on your page so that your audience is informed. This way people can reach out to connect with you, growing your network. Moreover, you can start exploring other career opportunities. There is a tab on LinkedIn called "Jobs." This can help you get a feel for what's out there and what you need to know going into the interview process.

What if you want to become an entrepreneur in life after sports, and don't necessarily want to work in a traditional job setting? Exploring this section doesn't necessarily mean you have to be looking for a job, but you *can* explore different roles and see what options there might be for internships. This can help you meet more people, expand your knowledge about a certain industry, and even help you figure out the inner-workings of a company. But if you are seriously looking for a job, this is the perfect opportunity to apply for roles that you know you might be interested in. You can even position your career interests to reflect which job recommendations might work best for you. With tons of companies looking for applicants that have the natural intangibles that most athletes have, LinkedIn is the prime location to display why you'd be perfect for them to hire.

The most important thing you should be doing is connecting with people and finding potential partners—and at the end of the day, LinkedIn is still a social platform. You can literally search for executives, directors, managers, owners, and any type of leader from almost any company in the world. It is hands down the easiest way for an athlete to contact and interact with decision-makers or collaboration partners for potential side projects like charity or non-profit work, public speaking engagements, or business partnerships. If you take advantage of every opportunity to do so—I promise it will pay off in the long run.

Every single athlete regardless of what sport they play should be utilizing LinkedIn, early in their career. It's not just for student-athletes who are transitioning into corporate roles and it's not just for professional athletes looking to partner with different brands. Every athlete from any sport can benefit from the multiple options that LinkedIn provides. This is so vital because this social media platform, more than others, can educate athletes on the various career choices they have for life after sports. It prepares them for that next step before they are ready to actually take it. It allows them to connect and meet people who will have a vested interest in helping them transition. And using it the right way almost guarantees a more effective and seamless transition.

Taking the proper steps to ensure that you will be ready to move on in life after sports can start in many different ways, but making sure that people see and recognize that you're not just an athlete is a crucial one. Using LinkedIn will prevent you from having a singular mindset and allow you to see that you can be more than just an athlete. The journey to life after sports can be difficult and long, but the sooner that you prove to yourself that you are worth more, the easier it will be in the long run.

YOUTUBE

According to a *Business Insider* article, YouTube is officially bigger than Gmail, and nearly as big as Facebook, with over 1.8 billion monthly logged-in users. The video viewing platform started in 2005, and has only continued to grow at an incredible rate ever since. There isn't another platform that can compete with YouTube for viewership of long-form video content.

Vlogging has become a major phenomenon in the past several years. Some of the early and most known Vloggers from YouTube are now global celebrities. Even how-to tutorials and DIY (do it yourself) videos are attracting millions of views every day. These stats reveal the power behind YouTube, and illustrates how consumers are turning to video for entertainment and education. YouTube may be the most impactful platform for any athlete looking to build their personal brand, depending on your strengths and personality. I've listed the four main reasons why it is important and will continue to be in the future.

1. VIDEO CONTENT IS PARAMOUNT.

Video has been proven over the years to command consumers' attention more than anything else. In a world where we all face so many distractions, having engaging, original long-form or short-form video content can be the difference between people following and consuming your content, or watching a game on ESPN or scrolling through Instagram. Attention is not growing; it's just slowly shifting, so figuring out how to capture it within your target audience is very important.

Also, due to accessibility, video can be easily consumed on a variety of devices and with more convenience than television. More and more people are using apps on their phones and tablets to watch their favorite shows, and tune into their favorite influencers' daily uploads. There is a land grab of opportunity for athletes who already have a following and those who want more people following them. All you have to do is figure out what works best for you when coming up with a strategy for your video content.

2. IT CAN EASILY BE REPURPOSED AND REDISTRIBUTED.

Video is pillar content. You can create a piece of long-form video content that can be used on YouTube, which can then be broken down into smaller pieces you can use on Instagram, Twitter, Facebook, and other platforms. You can even repurpose and transcribe it into blog posts and articles for LinkedIn and *Medium* and turn the audio into a podcast as well.

Of course, you might need a team or someone to help you with this, but it allows you to essentially make one big piece of content and redistribute it across multiple mediums without having to recreate anything or think of something brand new. As an athlete, you're already extremely busy, and doing this saves you a ton of time in building your brand. Video content is so powerful because it is the only form of content that allows you to do this.

3. YOU CAN RECORD A REGULAR DAY IN YOUR LIFE.

Fifteen years ago, it would have been ridiculous to think that people could actually make a substantial living by filming and documenting their entire day. Now, it doesn't really seem that crazy at all. In fact, everyone thinks that they can do it (even though not everyone can). As an athlete, especially at the pro level, you have an advantage because people are genuinely interested in your day-to-day life.

Imagine if LeBron James or Cristiano Renaldo had someone following them around day in and day out, filming their every move. Think about how many people would tune-in and how LeBron and Cristiano could leverage this attention. It would probably be billions of people. Athletes of their stature don't necessarily need to do this because they're at the absolute pinnacle of their sport, but any middle- or low-tier professional athlete could just document a regular day in their life and people would absolutely engage with this type of content. Just look at Gary Vaynerchuk, who epitomizes this concept and the others who have followed suit.

4. IT VISUALLY ALLOWS PEOPLE TO SEE THE REAL YOU.

I talk all the time about how we are first perceived online, then we are judged in person. If you can't get in front of everyone to show them "the real you," then video content is your next best bet. You can kind of hide behind a few blog posts. Audio is more personable than blogging, but people can't see your reactions or expressions when you say certain things. With video, as long as you're being your authentic self, people will get a full 360-degree view of who you are and what you're like. It's just like having an in-person interaction, digitally.

Adding video content and distributing it on YouTube can attract an audience that resonates with you and your lifestyle. When you allow people to see the most authentic form of who you are up close, you give them the immediate opportunity to like you—or not. Remember, your goal isn't to make everyone like you. Your goal is to make some people like you a lot and stay loyal to you forever, especially whenever you head into life after sports.

Video is still only at the beginning of its prominence. Even though YouTube has been around for many years now, we are really just starting to see the true potential with people tapping into it from all different industries. Creatives and innovators are emerging from everywhere talking and creating videos about everything from tech products to slime. There is ample opportunity for anyone to create what they're passionate about and use YouTube to show the world and connect with other people who are passionate about it too. Don't underestimate the power of YouTube and what it can do to create opportunities that can last you well after your athletic career.

PODCASTING

While podcasting isn't necessarily a social media platform, I thought it was necessary to talk about how you can use it to build your brand and following. In the past five to ten years, podcasting has become an extremely popular and fast-growing form of media. There have been individuals who have virtually come out of nowhere to create powerful brands by building their audience through starting their own podcasts. Influencers and entrepreneurs such as John Dumas and Lewis Howes, who is ironically a former professional athlete, have generated millions of dollars (we'll discuss how later) and worldwide fans through their podcasts and they are not the only ones who have been able to create a career from behind the mic.

Before anything else, you have to really understand why podcasting has grown so much. The main reason is that it's passive content consumption. People choose to consume podcasts over other forms of media because it's easy and saves them time. Reading this book requires you to sit down and be fully engaged in what I'm conveying to you whereas a podcast doesn't. Watching a video requires your full attention, a podcast does not.

Listening to podcasts allows us to handle other obligations such as going to the gym, running errands, and being productive in some way while still being entertained and/or gaining knowledge. You're also able to build an intimate connection with people with a podcast with virtually no barriers to entry. Hearing someone talk about their experiences, or tell a story is powerful because you can gauge their tone and feel the emotion. You can build a strong community around that.

Lastly, podcasts have a long shelf life and no time constraints. You can listen to an episode as many times as you want, whenever you want. If you run your own podcast, you decide how long you want it to be and how many episodes you want to put out. At the end of the day, podcasting is just modern-day radio, but with the number of shows that are out there, we can literally hear about any topic we want from people that we look up to. The networks don't control what we hear—with podcasts, we now have complete control.

There is no time like the present for athletes to get involved.

The beauty of starting a podcast as an athlete is that in most cases, you don't have to build a following with it. You can just use the fan base you already have and simply ask them to listen. Even the athletes who barely get off the bench have some type of fan base that would probably listen to their show. Podcasting can elevate that fan base beyond what you can imagine. It can be instrumental in helping an athlete reach new demographics plus deepen the relationships they already have.

For example, say an athlete wanted to start an interview-based podcast for an hour, just once a week, with athletes from other sports on their workout routines, diet, and training methods. Not only will this give listeners a firsthand perspective on the lives of both athletes, it will help both of them gain exposure to a new market in a different sport, not to mention improve their media and interviewing skills.

Josh Hart, who currently plays in the NBA for the New Orleans Pelicans, started an interview-based podcast along with his best friend Matt Hillman. They interview celebrities, influencers, and other athletes every week. In just the first week alone they cracked the top ten for all sports podcasts on iTunes. Now, Josh has been able to amplify his brand and build more relationships with people from various industries. They also got a sponsorship deal with Venmo. Any athlete can easily host their own podcast, talking about whatever they want.

They can mix it up and do one-on-ones, Q&As, and a variety of other things. It all depends on the personality of the athlete, their interests, and how they want to go about it. A podcast is probably one of the easiest ways for any athlete to gain more brand recognition and awareness. Not to mention that starting a podcast is extremely easy to do, which is great news for any athlete who wants to get in the game.

Before you jump in headfirst, you have to first figure out what you want to talk about, who your current target audience consists of, how long and how frequent each episode will be, and what the format will be. You have to lay this out before doing anything else because even though you already have fans, you have to know your fans well enough to know why they should stick around and listen to you. As I said, there are hundreds of thousands of podcasts out there. Just being an athlete won't cut it if you suck. Give them something worth listening to and they'll continue to tune in and stay with you for the entire ride.

Once you have these things in order, you can get into the technical stuff, like purchasing a microphone, a pop-filter, headphones, and some type of editing software for your audio which is usually free. Then, you can get your cover art and choose your hosting platform. After that is done, then you're ready to record and possibly edit your first episode. The last thing you have to do is to upload it to iTunes,

SoundCloud, Spotify, Google Play, or any other platforms you want to promote it on. After all this is complete, then you're officially a podcaster. That's all it takes, and I promise it'll cost you less than $200.

When I started my podcast, *Players Point Podcast*, it literally took me one weekend to figure out what I needed to do to get it off the ground—and a week from when I published my first episode, I was featured on iTunes. That's a quick overview on how to get a podcast started and obviously, you might not get the hang of it that fast, but it really is that simple a concept.

There have already been other notable athletes who have started their own podcasts besides Josh Hart including CJ McCollum, who currently plays in the NBA for the Portland Trailblazers, JJ Redick, who currently plays for the New Orleans Pelicans in the NBA, and Arian Foster, former NFL and Houston Texan running back. Even the Philadelphia Eagles football team has made an effort to launch several podcasts around their team that cater to different topics for their fans.

Podcasting is a fairly new trend, but it's a trend that isn't slowing down anytime soon and all athletes should try to take advantage of it, whether or not they have any aspirations of being an analyst or broadcaster. Whether you want to do it for fun, practice your speaking skills, or to eventually monetize it over time, there are tons of opportunities to be found in podcasting.

Now that you have read through and understand how to utilize the benefits of each of these major social media platforms, I think it's time we dive into some things you should avoid. Knowing what to do with these platforms is major, but knowing what you should never do matters even more, when looking at crises and protecting your brand for the long-term.

CHAPTER 5

THINGS ATHLETES SHOULD NEVER DO ONLINE

Why is it that we've seen so many athletes get into trouble when it comes to social media and things that they put out on the internet? Every athlete nowadays is growing up with these platforms at their fingertips, so they should know how to use them and what they should and shouldn't post, right? They should know the difference between inappropriate content and acceptable content. They should know what's appropriate and what can damage their career for the rest of their life, right?

Wrong.

Michael Harris, a long-time business manager and brand consultant for celebrities and athletes compares social media to youth sports exposure camps. He says,

Social media is almost like AAU basketball. Exposure camps and tournaments expose your strengths and your weaknesses. Social media does that as well. It exposes some of your opinions, some of your hatred or anger and that can alienate you from different people and some of the decisions that they have to make about you because of you expressing yourself.

Athletes, young or old, might have a basic understanding of the importance of social media and how to utilize it effectively, but knowing what they shouldn't say is a different topic altogether. This is why we see some athletes shy away from using social media on a regular basis. They fear that they will get in trouble by posting something unbefitting, which then shows up on the news and in turn can get them fined, suspended, or reprimanded in some form. Coaches, agents, advisors, administrators, and even parents are warning student-athletes and professional athletes not to use social media in an effort to prevent that.

This is the wrong approach. It shouldn't be about preventing athletes from posting online out of fear of judgment, trouble, or criticism. Athletes just need to be educated on the nuances of these platforms. Hell, athlete or not, all of us could really use some Social Media 101 if we are being honest.

Athletes should be allowed to be transparent online as anyone should, but as with anything there are limits to what should be revealed—especially if you're someone who is in the spotlight 24/7. Since we do live in a highly connected world, literally anyone and everyone can have and voice their opinion, perspective, or point of view on anything that is going on in politics, culture, current events, etc. Everyone can easily become a critic and comment on everything that you do. So being knowledgeable about what you're doing and talking about it is another important part of maintaining a strong digital footprint.

Everyone can be heard on social media, but if we're talking about an athlete, celebrity, or person with a large following, there is always someone constantly paying very close attention to everything they do and say. There are literally people working at companies whose sole job is to monitor athletes' profiles just to see if they can catch them making a mistake on social media.

This is exactly why you have to pay close attention to your actions on social media because once they're exposed, they will follow you for the rest of your career and life. That's why it is so much more important for athletes to have a serious understanding of what not to do when it comes to social media. It is what the world has become focused on and being cognizant of this matters for everyone's future.

Athletes, like anyone else, can be opinionated and want to be heard especially when it comes to issues that they deeply care about. As an athlete on the collegiate or professional level, you have to be wise and pick and choose the right time to speak out. And when you do speak out, you have to think about how people might respond to what you're saying. It is a fine line, and we've seen what can happen when athletes cross it. But if you want people to see you in a positive light, you have to censor yourself in some ways.

THE THINGS ATHLETES SHOULD NEVER DO OR POST ON SOCIAL MEDIA

The number one thing that athletes should never do on social media is post racist, gender offensive, or sexually insensitive remarks, even if it's in a joking manner. In this day and age, racism, religious prejudice, and gender oppression are all extremely sensitive issues. Some might argue that they're practicing to be a comedian or that it was all in good humor, nevertheless it's a discussion that you might want to think twice about entering into. And this can be tricky to navigate, because there are certain things that are now seen as ordinary or normalized in society's eyes. Things that might not have been socially accepted years ago might be accepted now. And things that might have been socially accepted in the past might not be in today's world.

If you're ever unsure or feeling doubtful about putting something out there, even if you're just asking a question, it's better to lean toward not doing it—all it takes is for one person to see it in the wrong way. Remember that you have a large reach which could include a lot of kids, so social issues, politics, religion, and other current events are touchy subjects that can mislead young kids, turn off many of your followers, and dissuade brands from working with you. People all around you, on every platform, will have a lot to say on all sides about these topics. They'll debate about what's right and what's wrong, what should be legal and what should be illegal, and it can create a ton of friction at times. That friction might make it tempting to join in on the conversation and voice how you feel, but always think about your brand first and whether you're ready to deal with the repercussions that might come from it.

The last thing you want to be known as is the athlete who unintentionally made fun of a certain person based on their race, religion, sexual orientation, or gender even if you didn't mean to. In 2012, Greek Olympian Voula Papachristou was kicked off of her national team for mocking African migrants and expressing support for a far-right political party. She only posted one tweet, but now that one tweet will follow her for the rest of her life, not just her athletic career. She clearly failed to realize the severity of her actions and it will cost her a lot in the long run.

Even more recently, Josh Hader who plays for the Milwaukee Brewers of the MLB had old tweets of his resurface during MLB All-star weekend in 2018. Of those tweets, many were racist, homophobic, and misogynistic remarks all posted directly from his Twitter account. He responded by saying, "I was young, immature and stupid." Regardless of the fact that he owned up to his mistakes—which helped him save face, somewhat—these tweets will live forever and leave an indelible mark on his baseball career. There will forever be negative connotations associated with Josh Hader's name because of a few tweets he posted when he was a teenager.

Along with refraining from posting insensitive content, you should never post any personal content that you won't want people talking about down the road. You should never reveal any images or videos of you or others smoking, drinking, with naked women, or anything related that might come back to haunt you later. I'm not saying you shouldn't or can't have a good time, but do it within reason and understand that not everyone around you will have as much to lose as you do, or even have your best interest in mind for that matter.

There might even be some people in your circle who want you to mess up and do something wrong because of jealousy and envy. This happens frequently and you have to be aware of it at all times. If you have to think about whether or not a photo is potentially inappropriate, it probably is. If you have been tagged in a questionable photo on social media, adjust your privacy settings, and go so far as contacting the person to see if they would be willing to take it down.

Your brand matters, and whatever is in that photo will be a reflection of who you are and who you associate yourself with for the rest of your life.

What do you want kids, and even people in your family, to think about the person you are when no one is looking? You not only represent yourself, but you represent your teammates, your family, the organization you play for, and the coaches. The things you do are a direct reflection of those who have invested in your career as well. Your brand is your brand, but the actions you take and who you hang around plays into that. Like minds always associate with one another. If you're a doctor, then you're going to hang out with other doctors. If you're into fashion then you'll probably associate yourself with other people in fashion. When you're an athlete, of course you hang out with other athletes, but whether they are your teammates or your friends from way back, you have to ask yourself questions such as:

> *"Are these people a good reflection of what I want my brand to be about?"*

> *"Do these people have as much to lose as I do?"*

> *"Do they care about their career and reputation as much as I care about mine?"*

It might seem unfair or unreasonable, but this is what you

sign up for when you become an athlete. Another good rule of thumb is what happens in the locker room, stays in the locker room. This is ground rule number one. If something goes down in the locker room, like a fight after a tough loss or coaches cussing everyone out: One, don't record it and post it. Two, don't talk about it with anyone except the people who were in that room. You're a family and what happens in the family stays between the family, period. It doesn't matter who you're arguing with, which coach cussed you out, or who or what teammate is having personal problems. What happens behind those closed doors stays behind those closed doors at all times. Nothing should ever get tweeted, posted, or talked about outside of those walls.

During the 2017–2018 NBA season, the Golden State Warriors had a major meningitis scare throughout the organization. The entire team had to get vaccinated and even had to switch practice facilities to prevent contamination. No one outside of the team heard or knew about it and they went on to win another title—their second in a row. This is exactly how it needs to be at all times. This is how a world-class organization is run and part of the reason why they have been so successful throughout the past several years. What goes down between the team always stays between the team during the season.

And while some might have mixed feelings about this, I

always say that you should never go back and forth with a hater or fan on social media. Let's face it, everyone who is a sports fan thinks that their opinion is valid or right. Half of the people that comment, commentate, or spectate on sports haven't played any sport a day past high school. This is exactly why you shouldn't even care what people say about you or to you on social media. Let the haters hate. People are going to talk about you until the day you die, especially if you are someone in the limelight. Don't waste your time going back and forth with them because the most it'll do is backfire on you. Why even try to prove yourself? If anything, responding validates and gives life to their comments. When someone says something negative about you, it says more about them than it does about you. You have to be able to let it die.

In November of 2019, Jermaine Whitehead, a former safety for the Cleveland Browns thought responding to people on Twitter with racial slurs and threatening remarks was a good idea after having a subpar performance during a Browns loss. In the blink of an eye, the Browns organization cut him and suspended his Twitter account before he left the locker room that same day quoting, "Jermaine White-head's social media posts following today's game were totally unacceptable and highly inappropriate." Another prime example: Kevin Durant made headlines for getting caught making a fake Twitter account to respond to his critics. Kevin Durant is one of the greatest athletes of all time so cutting him wasn't necessarily an option, but overall it'll end up being embarrassing and more times than not, always worse on the athlete's end.

"Never argue with a fool; onlookers may not be able to tell the difference."

—MARK TWAIN

Last but not least, just remember to never take playing sports either in college or for a living for granted. There are millions of people who want to be in your shoes. Have some class, and act like you know that you are fortunate to be in the position that you are in. When you do that, people not only respect you more as an athlete, but they respect you more as a person.

This is why athletes like Steph Curry are such great role models. You never see him getting into anything off the court and he keeps his values in order. People love him because he's been an underdog most of his life and a great basketball player, but at the same time, he is a community leader and a family man who has a great character and is known for being an outstanding human being. There's literally nothing bad you can say about the man, and that is why he makes the money he does on and off the court.

The bottom line is that you never know who's watching your moves, but know that someone is always watching. People are not only analyzing what you do on social media, they are seeing how you carry yourself in real life. Your body language, the way you dress, and the way you speak all matter equally when it comes to creating a brand for yourself. Social media is often the first thing that people think about when it comes to branding because of how much we use it. But your brand really starts before it even gets to social media. Social media is just an extension. It's simply a tool that magnifies who you really are.

Keep in mind that no matter where you go or what you do, as an athlete everything you do will be viewed under a microscope. And without a doubt, the negative things that you do will always be highlighted and broadcast before the positive things that you do. Let this be your guiding point before any post, picture, or tweet you put out in the world. All eyes are on you so you have to act accordingly. How do you want to be remembered? What do you want people to say about you when it is all said and done? What opportunities are you going to attract as you progress in your athletic career and life? The answers to these questions are all predicated on how you act on social media and in real life. Don't take it lightly. If you need help with a branding/social media strategy, don't hesitate to reach out to someone. It can make all of the difference in your career on and off the playing field.

CHAPTER 6

WHY EVERY ATHLETE NEEDS THEIR OWN PLATFORMS

Think about the last time that you heard a story that was told by someone other than the actual source. Now think about whether you had a chance to hear it from the actual source and compare the two stories that you heard. Was the first telling of the story slightly different from the source? Even though the differences might have been minor or insignificant, were there still details that were left out the second time you heard the story? Were there slight variations that could maybe change someone else's experience listening to it?

This is because perceptions, interpretations, or even the ability to listen can vary from individual to individual. The way one person hears or understands a story might be slightly, or even totally, different from the way you convey it. You might leave out a detail or two, which might seem small, but it could impact the way you tell a story when you explain it to someone else. And by doing this, it impacts the way that they tell the story to someone else and so on and so forth. This is a big reason why myths and stories passed down from generations change over time.

If you think about it, this is no different from your story as an athlete. Most of the time we are the main source for stories in sports. Journalists, reporters, coaches, agents, representatives, etc. all recognize us as "the horse's mouth," even though sometimes they might try to ask people close to us questions, or reference third-party sources to get their information and story details. When people go to sources other than the athletes themselves, they get information that might not be completely true, which can affect what is written or told about the athlete after the fact.

Over time, this just prompts athletes to be more reclusive with media and others, frustrated that their words are misconstrued by those around them. Things they might tell someone in private can come to surface. Even their actions can be taken out of context and their brand can be negatively affected because of misinterpretation, even if they have all the right intentions. When we tell our story through a media platform, or if we leave room for others to fill in our narrative with their own context, then that person might change it, sometimes without even realizing they did.

How they might have understood the story might not have been the way you wanted to explain it to them, but if you can completely control the context behind how you tell a story, it can remove all of the ambiguity, right? In other words, if you hear something directly from the source, and you have a relationship with that source, then there is very little room for miscommunication. That is exactly what a website can do for the modern-day athlete. Among a lot of other things, it can give them their voice back and create the exact story that they want to tell, without leaving room for vagueness or misinterpretation.

In essence, a website or digital platform that you own, further empowers your story and at the same time, allows you to voice your thoughts, opinions, and perspectives without any interference or interjection. This was the entire concept behind LeBron James creating the UNINTERRUPTED platform and Derek Jeter bringing *The Players' Tribune* to life. They saw a vision where athletes could talk about their lives and careers in the most authentic way imaginable.

The difference is that these platforms post content that athletes can't own outright. They have a stake in brand content deals and say-so as far as production, but not autonomous ownership. Nonetheless, if every athlete recognizes that they still hold the power when it comes to their voice and how they tell their story, then they still hold the leverage regardless of what others might say about them and the things that they do. When you're in the driver's seat, it doesn't matter who says what. I personally believe that every single athlete, from the moment that they reach the collegiate level and maybe even before, should have their own platform, not only for this reason but for many other key reasons that we'll dive into below.

WHY EVERY ATHLETE NEEDS THEIR OWN WEBSITE

The first thing a website does is give you the freedom to express yourself how you want and whenever you want. Along with social media, having a personal website allows you to be who you are, genuinely and authentically. You can express your thoughts, ideas, creativity, interests, and anything else you want to on your platform so that people can see you for who you really are. And no one can block or prevent you from doing so. There is no substitute for having a website in which you completely manage the content.

A website consolidates information for your fans, followers, and potential partners. It opens the door of transparency and lets those adoring fans fall in love with you even more than before. You can display your recent stats, in-game and outside of the game photos, what your goals and plans are for the upcoming season, etc. Your website is where your fans can go to get what they want in order to create a better relationship with you. When you own your platform, you're putting yourself in a position to gain more opportunities and possibilities because you're maintaining your relevance in the marketplace.

Having your own website provides a lot more options off of the playing field, even if you aren't thinking about that yet, because people can connect with you and keep up with you—as long as you are consistently updating it. For example, one of your biggest fans might be an executive for a Fortune 500 company who is interested in working with you or having you market their product. They can search your name, come across your website, and get an in-depth view of what you're about.

This happened to a professional female football player who I had on my podcast. She didn't make a lot of money as a professional football player, but by leveraging her athletic celebrity online, she gained opportunities to do commercials and brand consulting for a prominent doctor in her city. If you show people that you can market yourself online, as well as display your personality and character, they'll probably come knocking at your door sooner than you expect.

Lastly, you have to understand that ownership is everything. If something is yours, it's yours to keep and you can do whatever you want with it. Ownership will always be the way to go, whether it's something tangible or intellectual property. If Twitter, Instagram, Snapchat, and YouTube all went out of business tomorrow, a lot of celebrities, influencers, and athletes would lose tons of money and followers, and probably not know what to do next. If you have a platform that is completely yours, then your followers from these other platforms will still have somewhere to go and follow you no matter what happens to your social media profiles.

You can't own your profile on these other social media platforms, but you can own a domain name. Once you register for Instagram or LinkedIn, you give them permission to use your photos and data on that platform. It might seem like it's free, but what you're paying for is access to your privacy. Nothing in this world is free. Even though you might not look at the internet as real estate, that's exactly what it can be compared to. When you completely rely on these other platforms to generate business and opportunities for you, you are still at the mercy of their power, and essentially renting from them.

If Instagram wanted to delete your profile, they could. If Twitter wanted to ban you for a week, they could. If LinkedIn wanted to suspend you from posting, they could do it in a heartbeat. Those things probably won't happen to you, but they very well could. The point is that when you have your own website, you call the shots. If you own it, then who can take it from you? This is all part of the personal branding game that you have to capitalize on even before your athletic career really takes off.

You should be trying to capitalize on everything you can in the personal branding game. At the end of the day, that's all that any of this is and if you play the game right, not only do you win, but everyone wins. Playing the game includes owning your platforms, and promoting your thoughts and interests through them. It involves knowing how to implement different tactics, strategies, and just flat out being a good person in every aspect of the word. Bring something to the table, whether that's a following, great ideas for content, or charisma and personality. A website is one of the starting points when creating an online presence and a huge factor in whether or not you will actually have options outside of the sport that you play. Now that you have an understanding of why ownership online is important, we can address a few important points that go along with it.

WHY EMAIL MARKETING MATTERS

An extremely underrated marketing tool that most athletes don't take advantage of is email marketing. You're probably reading this thinking, "Why and when would I have the time to email anybody?" Hear me out for a second though. Email marketing became popular at the height of the internet boom in the early 2000s. Back then, if an email went out, almost 90 percent of people would open it because that form of marketing was so new to people. It didn't matter who it came from or what time of day it was sent. But now things have changed.

People are way too occupied with everything else going on in life to worry about email blasts or offerings. Open rates for emails are much lower than they used to be because it isn't a new concept anymore. We just don't care because our inboxes are already flooded with unsolicited emails on a daily basis—unless it comes from someone we really want to hear from.

Now imagine you're a freshman in high school. What if you got a direct email from Julian Edelman? Giannis Antetokounmpo? Mookie Betts? What if each week, they sent you emails for chances to win free gear or tickets, come to meet ups, or invitations to jump on FaceTime calls with them? Think about how excited you'd be at the possibility of actually communicating with them, one-on-one.

Now think about the kids and young athletes who look up to you now. Whether you're in college or a professional, there's a fan out there who would love to see your name pop up in an email. That is the power of personalized emails from athletes. It creates a stronger bond with the people who adore you. Plus almost no other athlete is taking advantage of this right now, so why not be the one to try to bring back an old trend that has endless potential?

HUMANIZING THE ATHLETE

Many athletes are looked at by other people as being superhuman. There are some who think that athletes are special or different from the rest of the population solely because of their athletic ability. They think that athletes don't experience the same things as the rest of us because they are so "powerful," "indestructible," and "competitive." As athletes who have reached the highest levels, it's easy to get caught up in the flattery and admiration, but at the end of the day, you know that you are human just like everyone else.

You experience pain, anger, fear, and fatigue. You have bad days and good days just like everyone else. The good thing is that you don't have to put on a persona or mask these things. In this era, it is actually good to humanize yourself. When you humanize yourself and show that you are just like the rest of the world, people gravitate to you in more ways than you could ever imagine. Why do you think the celebrities who own up to their scandals or embarrassing moments actually come out even more praised than before? It's because we forgive people for recognizing that they are human and that they make mistakes.

A great example of this is Michael Phelps—arguably the greatest Olympic swimmer of all time. After breaking Mark Spitz's seemingly unbreakable mark at the 2008 Summer Games, Michael Phelps was caught on camera smoking weed from a pipe at a University of South Carolina party. He later went to say, "I engaged in behavior which was regrettable and demonstrated bad judgment…I'm 23 years old and despite the successes I've had in the pool, I acted in a youthful and inappropriate way, not in a manner people have come to expect from me. For this, I am sorry. I promise my fans and the public it will not happen again."

He used his voice to release this statement, and by jumping on the situation quickly, he was able to rectify the situation somewhat and gain forgiveness from his fans. Depending on the context and gravity of the event, people realize that you will make mistakes, especially when you're in the spotlight. What they really want to know is: Can you own up to your bullshit? Can you admit when you're wrong and have the courage to say so out loud? When you humanize yourself and tell the true story in your words, sometimes your brand can be positively affected in the long-run. Don't pretend like you're not human, because at the core you're just like everyone else.

INVESTING IN LONG-TERM OWNERSHIP

We all know that media as a whole completely controls our lives, and the viewpoint of the world. As beneficial as it is for athletes to tell their stories through other media platforms, it is ten times more important for them to own and create content themselves because of one word: leverage.

Let me start by saying, this isn't a knock on what any other company is doing to help athletes by any means. In fact, I truly believe that without companies like *The Players' Tribune* and UNINTERRUPTED at the forefront of athlete storytelling, there wouldn't be as much of an emphasis on athletes controlling their own narrative. Nonetheless, one-off videos, podcasts, or stories are rarely enough to stay relevant in today's world.

There is just too much commotion in the world and it's not just about whose voice can stand out uniquely, it's also about who's the loudest. Just as quickly as someone reads your story on one of these publications, they can forget it and be on to the next athlete. You have to have quality and quantity and to do this, you have to be in complete control of what you're putting out into the world. You're not only competing with the athlete next to you, but you're also competing with the likes of ESPN, Bleacher Report, Bar Stool Sports, ESports, etc.

Everyone is vying for consumers' attention and athletes can have first dibs if they can break through constantly and consistently. Now, if you are a top twenty to thirty athlete in your respective sport, then all of this might not really pertain to you, but if you fall further down the line, you really have to think long and hard about your brand and how you want to be viewed in the future. You have to ask yourself questions such as:

Am I putting myself in a position for my story to be remembered?

Am I building authentic relationships with my fans and followers?

Am I connecting on a deeper level and getting people to react to the content that I put out?

Will I even matter once my athletic career is over?

If most of these answers are "No" then it might be time to invest in branding and marketing on a higher level. And this might mean hiring a team, a company, or even an individual to help you strategize, create, and distribute. I know many athletes might be apprehensive about the ROI, or they might think they don't have enough money to afford a team or this type of service. However, if you do invest in yourself and your brand, the return can and will be astronomical.

"You get what you pay for."

Not only will you be able to generate revenue in a multitude of ways, but you'll also be able to build more relationships and have more options outside of your sport than you ever imagined. Don't believe me? Look at what lacrosse star Paul Rabil has been able to do. Look at the media empires that Kevin Durant and Steph Curry are building. Even look at former Chicago Bulls guard, Jay Williams and how he's been able to build his brand and transition despite playing just one year in the NBA. They are living proof that athletes who invest in their name, and their brand, ultimately see results.

You might not be in a position to really level up on your brand and hire people, but you can't disregard it. Even starting on a low-level, like getting out your phone, shooting a short video talking about the other things you're passionate about outside of your sport, and posting it on Instagram or Twitter, is a start. You have to start building your foundation if you haven't already.

This is about content and media, but more importantly, it's about owning your IP and using it in the way that you want to. The time is now to own your platform, image, and likeness. We all know how small the window is for any athlete, so why would you wait when all of this access is at your fingertips?

CHAPTER 7

THE POTENTIAL PATHS TO PROFIT

We wouldn't be having this entire discussion about building your personal brand in the first place if there wasn't some type of way to potentially monetize it or do something else with it. We don't build brands for the sake of building brands. We do it because it's a means to a bigger end. That's what this chapter is all about. The opportunities for you to make money with your brand can come in many different ways as a pro athlete. In writing this book, I've realized that we might be on the brink of every collegiate athlete having the chance the make money with their image and likeness (hopefully sooner than later) which will be a game changer, but that's not the case yet.

When it comes to monetary opportunities, a lot of athletes either don't know how to find them or are too preoccupied to know when they slap them right in the face. I was the same way for so long, and it's really not your fault. Starting from our amateur years, we've all been conditioned to look at our sport as our sole focus. And this isn't necessarily bad. It should be the number one focus if you're trying to play at a high level. At the same time, by having this singular focus, you can miss out on the things around you that could have a great effect on your life.

This goes for any athlete, whether you're playing overseas in a small city in a country in Europe, or if you're playing for the best team in the NFL. You can have a lot of potential monetary opportunities, whether they come right to you or you have to create them yourself (we'll also address collegiate athletes and the non-monetary opportunities they can create). Keeping an open mind to the different things that might come your way is important. You have to realize that this is a world of abundance and prosperity. No matter what you want outside of a successful athletic career, I can almost guarantee that there is no shortage of opportunities to get it.

Being an athlete is your number one job, and when you're a professional, it's the job that puts the food on the table. Nevertheless, it's a job that won't pay you forever so while you do have to perform and do well to sustain your athletic career, you have to keep this fact in the back of your mind every day. It can take a very long time to get to the professional level, and even the collegiate level, but in less than a quarter of that time, your career can be over. In the blink of an eye, the opportunities that you might have had as an athlete aren't there.

Many athletes make the mistake of sitting back and waiting for money-making opportunities to come to them. Some of those opportunities might in fact come without you having to do anything, but for the average athlete, most of them won't. Just like any other business model, to maximize growth and success you have to get out there and bring about those opportunities for yourself. Focusing on your online and offline identity will strengthen your fan following, which can result in a "no-brainer" business proposition to a sponsor company, partnership, or brand, but if you can sell yourself then you will be miles ahead of other athletes who are vying for the same deals.

The sports and entertainment industry is full of athlete brand managers, marketing agencies, and even independent consultants who can help find other outside revenue-generating opportunities for you. They might take a cut, but if you find the right person who knows what they're doing—the advice and guidance you receive in this process can be invaluable going forward.

As an athlete, you can now become a global icon if you really want to. You can become the most notable athlete outside of the game even if you aren't necessarily the most talented in it. If you're willing to work hard enough outside of your sport, there are no limits to your success. Monetizing your brand as an athlete doesn't have to be complicated—you just have to be committed and I promise you'll start to see the opportunities line up for you.

PODCASTING REVENUE

We've already discussed why and how podcasting has become increasingly popular within the last several years. And wherever there's a new trend and attraction, there's potential to make money with it. Since podcasts are extremely easy to set up and affordable to start, you can see a huge return if you monetize it in the right ways.

Even with everything you have on your plate, if you just host a podcast once a week, or even once a month, it can build a stronger unity amongst your fans. As your podcast grows, you can monetize it in a variety of ways. You could have companies advertise their products and services in between your episodes on a CPM, or cost-per-thousand basis, which is generally priced as follows:

- $18 per 1,000 downloads for a 15-second "pre-roll" mention at the beginning of your show.
- $25 per 1,000 downloads for a 60-second "mid-roll" mention during the middle of your show.

These metrics might have already changed by the time you read this and undoubtedly will change over the next several years as podcasting grows, but typically this is what sponsored posts on a podcast would look like, and how much you could make by doing it on a consistent basis. Another option is to sell your own products (t-shirts, socks, jerseys, etc.) by setting up a website. You just have to redirect customers to that link through short promotions throughout your podcast.

You could also create a membership portal or receive donations for exclusive and additional content, which can be done through websites like Patreon, or you could coordinate with a big-time podcasting network for revenue sharing deals. The last major way to make money with podcasts is affiliate sales, and we'll talk about this in the next method of the paths to profit.

Venture capitalists and investors are starting to pour millions of dollars into major podcast networks that are creating original shows. This is a precursor to how much money will be up for grabs for the top podcasters. For a podcast to be monetized, all you need is a unique idea and a little time to get it off the ground. After you've built up a substantial community and trust with your listeners, there will be more and more ways to make money with it in the near future.

AFFILIATE MARKETING

This is a concept that a lot of athletes might not be too familiar with, but can be very profitable because of the influence athletes have over specific demographics or groups of people. Affiliate marketing is selling another company's product for a percentage of that sale. Lots of companies offer the possibility to earn money with product endorsement, because it is a way to expand their brand without breaking their budget, and they can form relationships with people of influence.

Typically the company will give you a code or link that you can share with all your followers on social media to make purchases on your sponsor's website, and you get a small percentage of the purchases that are made from that link or code. The amount is somewhere between 10 to 20 percent of the wholesale price. Below is a great example from The Institute for Athlete Branding and Marketing of how affiliate marketing works, and how profitable it can be for some of the most well-known athletes.

Example:

> Imagine LeBron James, who is already a huge wine aficionado and has over 100 million social media followers, enrolls in Wine.com's affiliate program. Then, imagine LeBron publishes a blog post on his website about the top 10 bottles of wine he recommends, with affiliate links to purchase each one on Wine.com.

Lastly, imagine this blog post inspires half of one percent of LeBron's social media following—more than 500,000 people—to purchase at least one of these bottles of wine, with an average purchase order of $20. Assuming LeBron retains a modest four percent of the total sales for being a member of Wine.com's affiliate program, he would generate around $400,000 (about the same amount of money he earns per NBA game) for publishing just one blog post. And again, that's just one blog post. Now, imagine LeBron makes a strategic decision to join a few more affiliate programs (e.g. Amazon Associates Program) and runs one affiliate "promotion" (blog post) per month. For less than a week's worth of work, that's an additional $5 million in annual, scalable, almost completely passive income.

Not every athlete has the prominence or following that Lebron James does obviously, but even if you're a second round NBA or NFL draft pick from the University of Maryland for example, and you have a substantial social media following of let's say 150,000 people, becoming an affiliate for a company is a great way to make some dollars on top of your playing salary. And if you have enough of a relationship with your consumers, then that take home can equal almost as much as your annual salary with your team. Something to think about.

PRODUCT OR MERCHANDISE LINE

With e-commerce websites like Shopify and websites where

you can create your own marketing place like Amazon, eBay, and Etsy, athletes can go directly to the end-consumer selling different types of products while eliminating the middleman completely. Athletes can design, create, and ship their own products and clothing line straight from their own platforms. This is so powerful because many athletes have thousands of fans who would love to purchase gear, merchandise, or any type of product directly from them rather than other companies who stock them.

A majority of sports fans love memorabilia and clothes that feature their favorite team or player on it. Many of them would pay a lot to get it too. Brandon Steiner, founder of Steiner Sports Marketing, made his fortune through his relationships with athletes and selling top-notch sports memorabilia. He has probably sold somewhere around the same amount as some organizations have throughout his forty-plus-year career in the industry.

By going straight to the consumer, you completely remove any friction or need for another brand to be involved, which will help you take complete control of the revenue stream for your brand. If you're passionate about design, fashion, or customization, this is also a really good way to hone your skills for the business side of the industry. Starting your own line or product-based business is relatively easy to launch and can have a high return if you have a strong creative side.

YOUTUBE CHANNEL OR VLOG

Previously, I mentioned how having a Vlog gives your fans an inside look at your life. Every fan wants to know what their favorite athlete does when they aren't playing their sport. Once you create enough videos and build a substantial subscriber list, that's when the money can start rolling in.

Through ad revenue and sponsorship dollars, many YouTubers have been able to make a significant amount of money. Ryan Kaji, host of the popular YouTube show "Ryan's Toy Review" on YouTube, has over 20 million subscribers and generates $11 million a year through his channel as a seven-year-old. It's amazing to think that a simple show on YouTube where a kid can review the best toys for other kids makes millions of dollars per year.

Examples like that are the exception, but they show what's possible when it comes to consistency and building an audience. A more relevant example would be Donald De La Haye, former kicker for the University of Central Florida football team. In 2017, he was ruled ineligible by the NCAA and kicked off the team for attempting to monetize his YouTube videos, which he started posting in 2015. As the poster boy for rebellious NCAA athletes, Donald was very outspoken and took to the internet to voice his arguments for why student-athletes should be able to receive money for their entrepreneurial efforts. Many stood behind

De La Haye, and his case was instrumental in shifting the conversation about why college athletes should be able to monetize their personal brands.

In the midst of all this, not being able to play football on scholarship any longer, he continued to post videos and other forms of content that has generated hundreds of thousands of views on YouTube, Instagram, and other forms of social media. Currently, he is still keeping up with his YouTube channel and has over 2 million subscribers while also pursuing a pro football career in the Canadian Football League. Donald De La Haye sacrificed his scholarship for the belief that all athletes should have the ability to make money with their image and likeness—incredibly commendable to say the least.

TRADITIONAL SPONSORSHIPS AND ENDORSEMENTS

This is probably one of the most common ways that athletes envision themselves making money outside of their sport. Promoting a company's product and getting paid to do it frankly seems too good to be true. Though there are a lot of things that go into sponsorships and endorsements behind the scenes, especially on the creative side, all athletes can use their relevance and awareness to partner with brands who align with what they believe in. In turn, athletes can receive revenue through social media posts and other forms of content creation.

The challenge with finding sponsorships and endorsements is that athletes are now competing with thousands of other influencers, travel bloggers, models, and celebrities on social media who want the same deals. The market is very saturated because everyone is looking to get paid to post pictures online. That right there is the dream job for a lot of people. It's getting even more complicated because now companies are seeking out influencers and ambassadors who have a niche following that appeals to the ROI of that particular brand.

In other words, it doesn't really matter if you have hundreds of thousands of followers if they aren't the people that company is trying to reach. It's no longer just about volume and large numbers. Because the market is so crowded, you now have to intentionally understand what your brand is about in addition to the business side. You have to know the audience that you're attracting and appealing to, then you have to go out and hunt for those opportunities to get paid with the right companies or else you're wasting your time. To make it a little easier for you, I've laid out step by step how to approach getting the right deals to post on social media.

The first step to getting paid to post on social media is to *know what you want and why you want it*. Every athlete says that they want to get sponsored. Most people don't know what that means or what it involves exactly. As an athlete you know the importance of goal setting. The more specific the goal is, the more likely you are to achieve it. You have to use the same logic to find a sponsor to pay you. You also have to get in tune with your "Why?" because it'll be hard to get deals that are actually worth the time and money. To push through the no's you need to have a powerful enough reason to keep trying to break through when times get difficult and you feel like you don't want to keep pitching. It's always worth it if you're strong enough to endure.

Next, you have to understand the different levels of sponsorship and what they look like. There are several different types of sponsorships for athletes. At the very beginning of your career, a lot of sponsors will try to give you discounted gear or free equipment. This is because they either don't know your value as an athlete yet or they want to see how your career evolves over the next couple of years. Don't be discouraged because this will likely change over time as your reputation grows and your value as an athlete increases. You just have to perform and do the things that you are supposed to do on and off the playing field. Then, as you become more well-known, you will not only receive the free or discounted gear, but also financial compensation and opportunities to have some of your miscellaneous expenses covered, depending on what they are. The final stage or level of sponsorship will usually include free gear and equipment as well as a monthly or yearly salary.

Of course, not all sponsorship deals are equal and won't be structured like the previous examples every single time. But by moving up the ranks of sponsorship levels, whatever they might be, you will slowly gain credibility, experience, and knowledge that will help you with future deals and partnerships. Just like any athletic career, it's all about moving up the ladder to bigger and better opportunities. As your athletic career grows, your personal brand should grow with it.

After you have a strong understanding of what sponsorship deals are about, as well as the different levels, you should identify potential sponsorships and brand partnerships and list them accordingly. **This is crucial. You don't want to waste your time pitching to the wrong company.** It's all about the right fit. Take some time and think about what kind of sponsors you could imagine yourself working with. What kind of companies are sponsoring your sport now? What companies fit your personality and brand persona? Companies nowadays look at the bigger picture, so try to be known for something outside of your sport. Check out other industries, or even companies in your local community. You have to be extremely creative and think outside the box because opportunities are all around you.

After you've identified potential companies that you want to partner with, you have to build a great pitch and proposal to bring to the table. You have to be able to show them your value and why you are a great fit to promote their product or service. There will be a lot of companies and brands that tell you they're not interested, or that they don't have the budget for you. Sometimes you have to keep pushing and keep trying. Some brands will even try to lowball you and act like they don't have the money to pay you what you're asking for, but never let that force you to settle or stop negotiating.

There are tons of templates and ideas on the internet for drafting a solid proposal. I recommend that you find a way to be creative and think about something that will separate you from other influencers and athletes who are trying to pitch them. While putting your own spin on it—make sure you do not create a large word document or a long presentation. That turns most companies off and they won't take the time to read all of it anyway. Lastly, remember you only need a "Yes" from the one key decision-maker or to reach someone in the marketing department. Also make sure you think about the following points when creating your proposal.

YOU ARE A MARKETING ASSET

Don't ever forget that companies are treating sponsorships as a marketing investment. **You** are representing and supporting the company that is sponsoring you so consider this at all times.

KNOW YOUR VALUE

This is something that many athletes continue to miss. Sometimes we simply don't know our own worth when we begin to leverage our impact off the playing field. Always remember that what you can do and bring to the table is special and unique. It took you years of practice and hard work to get to where you are now. Very few people have the skills, dedication, and the talent that you do. At the end of the day, why not get paid for something that you trained your entire life for if the opportunity presents itself?

STAND OUT

One lesson that you can learn from the top, world-class athletes is to stand out. We should all be grateful for our differences, and instead of trying to hide our uniqueness, we should embrace it. Standing out is why companies will like and connect with you. If you are exactly like the rest of the athletes who are trying to get the same deals, there is no reason why a company should pick you over them.

BE CONFIDENT

This is easier said than done, but it's time for all athletes to really up their self-esteem. Don't underestimate how far confidence can bring you. You are confident when it comes to your sport, but taking that confidence to the outside world is the challenge you have to face. Don't let a lack of confidence deter you from getting what you want. Even if you're nervous or uncertain about what you can get, be confident no matter what.

Last, but not least, you have to stay consistent with reaching out. Be as consistent as you are with your training and workouts. As I mentioned earlier, companies will try to turn you away, but don't get discouraged if you do not hear back from the companies you approach. Don't let anybody stop you or slow you down. You will find the right sponsors—when the time comes. This is a game of patient and persistence. "No" just means next opportunity.

SPEAKING ENGAGEMENTS

Athletes are highly respected in the communities that they play and live in, as well as the communities that they come from. Fans want to see athletes involved in community outreach, and who are giving back to good causes. Speaking engagements and special appearances are a great way to do both of those things. Organizations and companies will pay you to come out and speak about your experiences. Or you can give keynotes at charity events and schools. There are many athletes who also organize their own events and meet and greets, inviting people to come out to get autographs and pictures.

The best way to go about finding opportunities to speak is by utilizing your network, and posting on social media, letting people know that you are looking for those opportunities. Think about who can introduce you to people who are looking to have athletes speak, or who can directly book you themselves. Those people can be anyone including former administrators at your previous schools, or family friends.

If you're a pro athlete who has some tenure in your sport, you could possibly leverage your experience to speak at companies about topics such as leadership, teamwork, discipline, and other sports-relevant topics that companies can benefit from hearing. Plenty of athletes have made entire careers outside of their sport from speaking, including former NBA player Keyon Dooling and former NFL player Marques Odgen. This can earn you big bucks, especially if you won a lot during your career and built a good name within your sport. Even if you start off speaking for free, doing this allows you to develop a portfolio of engagements that you've done over time, which can be used to get more paying gigs.

Another thing to practice is telling your story or your overall message, and the key takeaways you want the audience to get from it. The more comfortable you get doing this and the clearer you are on why people should pay to listen to you, the higher your price can be. Practice in the mirror, or just spend thirty minutes every day going over what you would want to convey to the audience. Getting paid to speak is relatively easy once you've done it enough and put in the time. Like anything else, the more you practice speaking, the better you will become, and the more likely people will come to you over other athletes you might be competing for jobs with. Speaking, just like finding brand deals and endorsements, comes down to persistence and consistency. When you get the ball rolling in the speaking industry, you can reach a ton of people with your message and make some really good money long-term.

ANGEL INVESTING AND VENTURE CAPITAL

In the past several years, many athletes have started to try their hand at investing and venture capital. Some of them have managed to start their own funds during their playing career such as Derrick Morgan, now a former NFL defensive end, and Kevin Durant, superstar NBA forward for the Brooklyn Nets. Other athletes like Marques Colston, former New Orleans Saints wide receiver, and even Ryan Howard, former MLB first baseman, have gotten into it after their careers were finished and are now viewed as veterans in the industry.

Either way, venture capital is a great way to learn how to grow your money in addition to learning about the daily ins and outs of any business. If you're looking to invest and have the extra capital to do so, along with the right guidance and a little luck, you can multiply more than ten-fold the money you originally put in. It might take some time to see substantial gains but some people have made enough to retire with just one deal.

The single best piece of advice that I can give you is to leverage LinkedIn and find groups or people who work in the space. There are plenty of individuals who are carving out niches specifically with helping entertainers, celebrities, and current and former athletes transition into this field, such as Rashaun Williams, founder of Manhattan Venture Partners. Many of the investors and advisors in this space also offer a lot of free information through content on social media.

Do as much research as you can before you reach out to these people as they are extremely busy and might take some time to get back to you. Some might not even answer depending on what you ask, so be specific and make sure you're asking the right questions. The investing business is becoming more and more popular with athletes. But I highly recommend that you know what you're getting yourself into beforehand, and also be ready to lose any capital you plan on investing, because that's often what happens in this industry. There are very few companies that make big returns, so be prepared to roll the dice if this is what you're looking to get into.

GETTING A TRADITIONAL JOB

Getting a traditional job, or what we call a 9-to-5, might not be the first thing on the mind of most athletes, but it's something that most athletes will have to do once they stop playing their sport, especially those who don't make it to the pro level. The big question is, how can you use your personal brand to get a job? As an athlete, you're going to be coveted by most employers. The natural traits, skills, and intangibles that you develop through playing sports are ideal for any job in the real world. Whether you notice that you have these skills or not, you do, and by using your personal brand, which allows you to clearly and authentically present yourself and your story to a potential employer, you have a winning formula for future opportunities.

Let me tell you a quick story: My very first "real" job was working in a retail store. Not just any retail store, it was as a sales specialist for Apple. Now, if you're not familiar with Apple's job application and interview process, let me provide some insight into what it's like. Unless you get a recommendation, it's pretty damn hard to even be considered for a position in the first place, even though it's retail. And if you are considered, you have to go through a group interview with about five or six other applicants, all of whom are usually going for the exact same position. After that, you will have at least two or three other one-on-one interviews with hiring managers and people in other leadership positions. If you can get past all of this, then you finally have to participate in an intensive ten-hours-a-day training program for one weekend.

I had never been on a job interview in my life before this, and had absolutely zero work experience. But after going through all of that, I was one of two candidates left standing and got the job offer a few days later. I later found out once I resigned from the position that I was hired for two main reasons:

1. I was being my most genuine and authentic self throughout the entire interview process.

2. Even though I didn't have work experience, I was completely honest and told my story about what it was like being an athlete most of my life.

Being an athlete can always be an avenue to different things, if you allow it to. Most of us will have to work in some capacity and can't afford to sit and relax once we walk away from the game, but getting the right job and knowing how to use your brand to do so can be the difference between a successful transition and an unsuccessful transition. A lot of that involves you telling your story and most of all, being in tune with what your brand is about.

CHAPTER 8

HOW TO DEAL WITH JOURNALISTS, REPORTERS, AND THE MEDIA

While much of your brand creation happens online, it is also made through your day-to-day interactions with journalists, reporters, and the media. You could rely on your social media pages to grow your brand, and avoid doing interviews, but a good personal brand is really built through face-to-face dialogue. It's built through deep, intimate connections, not from behind a computer screen or iPhone. Dealing with journalists and reporters can be hard to do on a regular basis; however, it can pay dividends if you prepare and practice beforehand.

I don't want to seem cynical and make the media out to be

bad or manipulative, but sometimes it can appear that way from an athlete's standpoint. Journalists can turn you off and make you not want to deal with them at times. Looking from the other side of the fence now as a retired athlete, I understand that it's all about business, and most of them aren't trying to personally attack you. They just have to do what's best for themselves and their careers, regardless of how you might feel about it. Truthfully, we are all doing that. In order for journalists and reporters to advance their careers or keep their jobs, they have to tell and curate stories. If they don't have an enthralling narrative to create, tell, and sell to the public, they could be out the door looking for another job.

It's a fine line when it comes to media interviews as an athlete. For them it's all about ratings, clicks, and numbers and for you, it's about keeping up your positive perception in the public spotlight and getting the truth out there in your own words. Since it is required of you to deal with the media as an athlete, sometimes as early as high school, it is only right that you know how to deal with them properly.

I remember being in high school and making the Varsity team my junior year. The previous year I had played Junior Varsity and our Varsity team was ranked somewhere in the top five nationally on every major high school ranking outlet, including ESPN and *USA Today*. We were being seen on the national stage and I knew the rest of my high school career was going to involve us as a team, and individually, being featured in the spotlight. As high school athletes playing in the WCAC (Washington Catholic Athlete Conference), we were playing in arguably the most competitive conference in the country for high school basketball.

Every night, I was up against some of the top high school talent in the country, and our games drew crowds from all over the area. Everyone you can think of came through to see us play on any given night, including high major Division-I coaches, local music artists, politicians, and reporters from every major news outlet in the area. We were under constant scrutiny and if you were a sports fan in Washington, DC, then you knew who we were.

After every game, the media interviewed either me or one of the other top players on our team, but the one thing I noticed early on was that we never had any formal training on how to do this appropriately. No one ever told us how to engage and interact with the media. No one taught us what to say, what not to say, how to position ourselves, or even asked us whether or not we were comfortable talking to them. Whenever we were called for an interview, we just kind of went out there and did it without hesitancy or forewarning. It was expected of you to perform on the court and conduct yourself the right way with the media. They just presumed that we knew how to do it beforehand and, looking back, that seems nonsensical.

How in the world can you expect a sixteen- or seventeen-year-old high school athlete who has had no formal media training or knowledge of the media, to properly know how to do an interview in front of a camera, which will be broadcast across a major news channel for the entire city to see? Luckily none of us ended up on the blooper reel or embarrassed our team or school. But in recent years, I've watched a few interviews with high school athletes who completely bombed—taking their teammates down with them. I can't blame those athletes, because who is teaching them how to do this? Who is giving them the right tactics and advice when it comes to this? My guess is hardly anyone, so I'll take it upon myself to at least try to do so.

In the past, there have been many professional athletes who have been very candid and outspoken toward the media, believing that the media is out to get them or that they're trying to get them to slip up and say something that will make the front page. Players' issues with the media have become more apparent in recent years, especially due to the responses from superstar athletes such as Kevin Durant and James Harden. Don't ever forget that participation in media events is required as much as an "optional" workout is. Frankly, if you want to be a high-level athlete you have to acknowledge and accept that you will be dealing with the media for the entirety of your career.

When being interviewed, there are specific guidelines that

you should follow in order to refrain from saying something that can be detrimental to your team, coaches, or yourself. This section of the book is arranged to give you specific, actionable tips for things to do and not to do when interacting with a journalist or interviewer. One of the things I am asked the most as a former athlete is, "What would you do differently if...?" or "If you would have known [blank] how would you interact?"

I've come up with fifteen specific points for how any athlete can effectively deal with going through the interview process with a journalist or reporter. Some things you might already know and some you might not. Some might apply to your current level as an athlete and some might not. Some are about things you *should* do and some are about things you *shouldn't*. The bottom line is that all of these are things I wish I had known, or had been reinforced, so that I could have been more confident in dealing with the mainstream media—because all of this plays a part in the way people see you.

KEY TIPS FOR HOW TO INTERACT WITH JOURNALISTS OR THE MEDIA

1. **Do not feel obligated to answer every single question.** Not every question the media asks you can or should be answered. If for any reason you don't want to answer a question, you don't have to. Don't let them pressure you to answer. "I can't come up with an answer

to your question" is a completely acceptable response. You can also say, "I don't know" or "I don't think I can answer your question right now" or "I don't understand what you are asking." After telling a reporter that a question cannot be answered, nothing else needs to be said.

2. **You are also allowed to pause for a second before you say anything.** While it's never the best thing to keep the media waiting for any extended period of time, you have a right to pause before speaking if you need to. This gives you time to think for a second about your answer intently before blurting anything out.

3. **Call reporters by name.** It's a common courtesy to refer to a reporter by his or her name. By doing this, it personalizes your responses, emphasizing that a relationship exists between you and the reporter or interviewer, which can look good for your brand. But this is not necessarily a requirement. It's also cool if you don't know names or don't feel comfortable in this role.

4. **Never talk bad about an opponent or the referees.** Nothing is to be gained from saying bad things about an opponent. The public might like "trash talk," but it can be a poor reflection on you from the decision-makers' point of view. To be on the safe side, keep in mind that most people admire an athlete who shows respect for

his or her opponent and focuses on his or her team's performance rather than dwelling negatively on the opponent. The latter can show weakness or insecurity. Also, any negative comments about officiating will be interpreted by the public as excuses. I'm sure you already know that no one likes someone who makes excuses.

5. **Be cooperative.** This goes back to points that I made at the beginning of this chapter. At the end of the day, reporters need your comments for stories. If you make yourself available to answer their questions, they will appreciate it because it makes them look more professional. Don't be defensive or standoffish. Attitude is everything. Whenever possible, concentrate on being the "good guy" (or girl) who is above pettiness and unprofessional behavior. This builds integrity and enhances your credibility in the eyes of your audience. Most audiences are sophisticated enough to recognize rudeness in any form.

6. **Do not feel rushed or goaded into giving answers.** Speak clearly with the proper rhythm. Avoid using generic clichés. Listen to the question carefully and stay focused. Make sure you understand the question before you answer it. If you don't understand, ask for clarification or have the interviewer repeat the entire question, and if it still doesn't click, ask to move on as we mentioned in tip number one.

7. **Your personal appearance always counts for something.** Maintain good eye contact with the reporter and do not worry about the camera. Keep your voice strong and animated. The way you dress is the way you will be addressed. After the game, make sure you shower and dress appropriately. If you don't have the time—keep your game attire on.

8. **Remember to say, "thank you."** Your final actions in the interview may leave the strongest impression with the reporter. You should try to make every encounter a memorable one—chances are you will receive more favorable stories and attention in the future.

9. **Act ethically and never lie to a reporter.** It might not be against the law, but it is unethical for an athlete to be untruthful with members of the media. You should always answer questions as honestly as you can. And beyond this, you are under no obligation to volunteer any additional information even if you're asked for it. You are 100 percent responsible and in complete control of the information you give out.

10. **It's OK to give short answers.** Short and simple answers are the best because they are easy to quote. Answers with a central theme that is clear can prevent you from rambling for minutes. When answers drag on, the likelihood increases of being misquoted, your words

or phrases being taken out of context, or you saying something that was not intended for the media.

11. **Avoid using jargon or slang.** If you want to be an effective communicator, try not to use sports-specific terms. Whenever possible, stay conversational and use language that is clear, direct, and constructive. Don't use language that only you and your teammates use that few people living outside the white lines would understand. If you do happen to use slang, you have to be willing to explain it because the last thing you want is for a reporter to interpret it in a negative way, and explain it to the public that way.

12. **Never speak "off the record."** This type of statement can be interpreted as an open admission that you aren't always open and honest with people. Athletes who attempt to speak in private tones can appear to be dishonest and devious even if they aren't trying to be. Besides, there are no such things as "off the record" comments. Sooner or later, restricted information will be reported by the media and become a matter of public record.

13. **Never joke with a reporter if you don't know if they're joking back.** While some questions might appear funny, answers should always be serious. The tendency to joke or play around with a reporter is an

open invitation to controversy. You never know how they might respond or how your answer will appear in print or sound on the evening news.

14. **Keep your cool.** You shouldn't feel intimidated by cameras, bright lights, tape recorders, or microphones being pushed into your face. Try to disregard interruptions, differences in opinions, offensive language, stupid or accusatorial questions, so-called statements of facts, or reporters leaving in the middle of an answer. You should always "keep your cool" when pressure mounts just like in a game. Practice modesty in victory and self-control in defeat. In victory and defeat, the good communicator controls their emotions and language.

15. **Lastly, do not spend too much time talking about a negative or a loss.** Negative comments will forever make headlines. Audiences assimilate and remember negative information more accurately than positive information. Whenever possible, share positive accounts and information. Therefore, when the game ends, you should be encouraged to direct attention to (a) communicating the progress made and (b) the job of the team in the coming days. Words will never change the score or alter a game performance. Whenever possible, voice optimism with regard to the future.

16. **Bonus Tip: Always show support for your teammates**

and your school. Honor the natural bonds that exist in your relationships. You should respect and always have your teammates' back. Remain sensitive and never make negative remarks regarding others' performances. Finally, never appear on camera wearing another team's letters, logo, or colors. It may be an accepted practice on your team or in your organization, but it's in bad taste. Pride is expected and is demonstrated through the way an athlete speaks and appears in public.

There are a lot of different ways to handle the media and the way you do interviews, but these are the pieces of advice I wish I had been given during my playing career.

If you take anything at all from this—the most important thing is to be the athlete that your teammates, coaches, and parents would be proud to be associated with. Be the person that's bigger than all of the bullshit that might arise during your athletic career. There is nothing to be said about someone who shows up, does their job to the best of their ability, and doesn't complain or raise issues with others.

Be that person right there. Because we've all seen athletes do or say things in the face of the media that probably made the people closest to them ashamed to be associated with them. Don't ever do anything to embarrass yourself. Don't embarrass your team or coaches. Most of all, don't embarrass your family and the people who mean the most to you.

CHAPTER 9

ATHLETES, POLITICS, AND SOCIAL ISSUES

When you reach a certain point in your life—and maybe you're already there—you'll come to find that there are specific topics that people will tell you to never discuss or bring up in conversations. In my experience, the main ones include religion, money, and politics. These subjects are particularly sensitive for a lot of people to talk about, which is why most people avoid talking about them. It's not uncommon for these subjects to stir emotions and cause arguments; therefore, it's usually best to avoid them altogether unless that's the kind of thing you're aiming to achieve.

However, the role of politics in sports is something that can be unavoidable at times, especially in the current climate we've been living through. So what happens when sports and topics such as politics collide? What happens when a young athlete stands up for something that he or she believes in despite political or public backlash? What does an athlete do when their values and moral principles are confronted and tested through the sport they play? What do you do as an athlete in this case? Do you stand up for what you believe in? Do you sit back and accept the situation for whatever it might give rise to?

This can be an extremely difficult decision to make, because you have a reputation that you want to uphold. Taking a risk and fighting for something you feel strongly about could possibly put that reputation in jeopardy for the rest of your life. On the other end, you might feel so strongly about a political issue that everything in you is telling you to act on it. Could you honestly live with yourself if you deliberately decided to back down when that voice inside is telling you to fight back? Could your conscience subside? Would you be able to go on knowing that you could have made a historical difference if you had done what you felt was the right thing, despite having a brand to uphold?

While I don't expect any athlete to know how to answer these questions without giving it a lot of deep thought, these are certainly scenarios that you have to consider, especially as you move along in your athletic career. For the record, these are things that I've been asked about by other athletes, and have personally encountered in my athletic career. I was always told that the most important thing is to be educated and have insight into the causes you believe in. Now, I think it's bigger and deeper than that. The world is already complicated and only getting more challenging to navigate by the day. Any athlete can create change, but at what cost? It takes some serious courage and confidence within yourself to stand up when others might be afraid to.

The best advice I can give to any athlete is to not only be knowledgeable about what you're fighting for, but also to go all in when it comes time to fight any social issue or political issue that you feel strongly about. It's not enough to be aware. You have to be fully committed. If you're going to get your hands dirty—you have to be willing to make it part of your lifestyle. Here are a few examples of star athletes who leveraged the attention they had to make a social impact, while also maintaining their integrity and reputation within the process.

COLIN KAEPERNICK

During a preseason NFL game in 2016 as the San Francisco 49ers were playing against the Green Bay Packers, Colin Kaepernick, who was the quarterback for the 49ers at the time, made a gesture that not only changed the trajectory of his athletic career, but also brought the country to a standstill and further exposed the distant divide throughout America. That day, Colin Kaepernick began sitting during the national anthem to express his disdain for the unjust killings of multiple unarmed African Americans by law enforcement officers throughout the country. Throughout the next several weeks he began to kneel in silence during the anthem, garnering national attention. What was meant to be a simple demonstration to protest the racism and systematic oppression that has been going on in the country, turned out to be one of the greatest social justice movements that the NFL has ever seen.

From there he started a movement in which many other NFL players began to participate around the league. Some people stood with him. Many stood out against him and expressed their hatred for what he was doing. Even President Donald Trump began voicing his opinion on the protest by saying, "NFL owners should fire the players who kneel during the anthem," and went as far as calling them "sons of bitches." Colin didn't do this with the intention of building a larger platform than what he already had as an NFL player. He did it because he truly believed in his cause. To the fullest degree, he believed it was wrong to stand up and show pride in a flag for a country that oppresses minorities and people of color.

Ultimately this decision cost him his NFL career and livelihood. It's been years since he took that knee and he's only been able to have one workout opportunity to showcase his talent and have a chance at getting back into the NFL, despite being discriminated against for his beliefs. However, his brand has elevated to new heights. He has been supported by millions of people worldwide. Other celebrities have spoken out because of his actions. Other athletes have gone to Capitol Hill in Washington, DC, to voice their opinions. Even Nike designed an ad campaign with him which became one of the most successful campaigns in the company's history. He now has a different mission and purpose.

According to his website, he founded and fully funded the national Know Your Rights Camps to empower youth in their community and teach them various ways to interact with law enforcement, as well as self-empowerment and motivation. He also completed his Million Dollar Pledge, where he donated $1,000,000 of his own money to thirty-seven different organizations fighting for justice such as Assata's Daughters, Standing Rock, United We Dream, and more.

Whether intentional or not, Colin Kaepernick has given a voice to people who didn't have one before. Even though this might not have been what he really wanted or planned for, he will never need to play football again if he chooses not to, or if he doesn't get another chance. He has built a legacy for himself and has become more than just a football player. He has brought an awareness to a major issue that has affected communities nationwide. Most importantly, he has shown what happens when you stand up in the face of adversity and speak out on what you believe is right. When you build a brand based on strong convictions, it can have life-altering effects.

BRENDON AYANBADEJO

I had the pleasure of interviewing Brendon Ayanbadejo after I connected with him through Instagram. The very first thing I noticed about him and his brand was his love of fitness and how open and honest he was. For a former NFL linebacker, his passion for working out wasn't unusual, but what did strike me as something out of the ordinary was his passion for social equality, and same-sex marriage. As I dived deeper into his story and NFL career, I was amazed at how big an activist he was, and also the impact that he made during his football career and is still making today.

Brendon is an athlete who isn't just about talking the talk. He is all about walking the walk. He's been in the trenches for years trying to make a difference, which is something most people wouldn't know. His resiliency and dedication as an athlete was also unmatched. His career has taken him everywhere from getting signed as an undrafted free agent, to getting cut by multiple teams and having to play in the CFL (Canadian Football League), to finally winning a Super Bowl in 2012 with the Baltimore Ravens. Being a product of biracial parents and growing up in impoverished neighborhoods, he came from nothing and had to claw his way up to where he is today. Hearing his entire story was extremely eye-opening and intriguing to say the least.

To me, Brendon is the type of athlete that you don't come across every day. He knows his purpose and lives it. Activism isn't a front or facade for him. It's who he is and who he was raised to be. And it showed more than ever during the 2012–2013 NFL season. Brendon, who has always been very forthright on gay rights and same-sex marriage, received notice from Baltimore Ravens owner Steve Bisciotto, that Maryland delegate Emmett Burns, Jr. sent a letter quoting:

> Many of my constituents and your football supporters are appalled and aghast that a member of the Ravens Football Team would step into this controversial divide and try to sway public opinion one way or the other.

He went on to further say that basically Brendon should just "stick to football," and stop speaking out on issues that don't concern the game. Obviously Brendon wasn't going to do this at all. He responded by saying:

> Surprisingly, Steelers fans, Patriots fans, Bengals fans, Cowboys fans, people who don't even watch the NFL have all sent me messages saying that, "I now have a reason to watch football or even cheer for the Ravens because of your support for equality," so that feels good.

With support from the president and owner of the Baltimore Ravens, Brendon continued to leverage his name to fight inequality, naysayers, and critics like delegate Burns even though he was released from the Ravens after that season. He still uses his stage for the greater good and has been featured on national media channels such as the Huffington Post, CNN, and ESPN for what he has done outside of football.

His name might not be as recognized as other athletes who have stood up for injustice but his cause is just as important. Now, he will forever be respected by other athletes who are passionate about same-sex marriage and gay rights, all because he stood up for what he believed in despite being openly condemned by others.

MALCOLM JENKINS

If you happen to be discussing politics and legislation, Malcolm Jenkins is definitely the one athlete that you want to talk to. Along with Colin Kaepernick, Jenkins was one of the many NFL players who protested before NFL games to bring attention to racial inequality in America. But he didn't stop there. He was also one of the few guys who went down to Capitol Hill in Washington, DC, during the 2017 offseason to take further action.

While there, he met with legislators to discuss everything

from improving relationships between minority communities and the police and supporting programs to help inmates successfully re-enter their communities, to the unjust murders of multiple African Americans during that time. Since then, Malcolm has also started his own foundation called the Malcolm Jenkins Foundation, which focuses on helping the youth in underserved communities through workshops and programs. His work in the community has shown his dedication to impacting lives outside of football. Whether it's in the media or in public, he has never held back from discussing his concerns about a number of events that have transpired throughout the country.

Rarely do you see athletes taking such a strong stance during their playing career, much less taking time out of their busy schedule to actually meet with government officials about creating change. This is what makes Malcolm Jenkins so rare and inspiring. Obviously, there is always work to be done to improve the racial divide and injustice in America, but athletes like Malcolm Jenkins are at the frontlines, showing up and doing their part in multiple ways. Again it's not enough to talk about it—you have to live it as well.

MUHAMMAD ALI

Now we're talking about arguably the greatest boxer of all time. Formally known as Cassius Clay, Muhammad Ali has been praised as one of the most candid and commendable athletes to ever grace this planet. He always stood up for what he believed in regardless of what anyone else thought, which outweighed anything that he accomplished as a boxer.

He protested inequality and racial bias in America and fought for civil rights in a time where he could have been arrested or even killed just for being an African American. And during this time, there weren't a whole lot of African American athletes as big as him who did the same thing. Kareem Abdul-Jabber and Bill Russell come to mind, but most African American athletes who were constantly in the public eye didn't want to risk their career for the movement. Ali believed and took action when other people were afraid to. And he showed his belief on several occasions such as joining the Nation of Islam when they were one of the most despised religious groups of the 1960s. He also refused to fight in the Vietnam War saying that:

> My conscience won't let me go shoot my brother, or some darker people, or some poor hungry people in the mud for big powerful America. They never lynched me, they didn't put no dogs on me, they didn't rob me of my nationality, rape and kill my mother and father...Shoot them for what? How can I shoot them poor people? Just take me to jail.

If you are drafted, it is your obligation as an American to

fight. And as an African American if you defied the law, you were basically writing your own death sentence. Ali just didn't believe it was his war to fight in. He didn't care about the repercussions. He took a stand for something bigger than himself. Even after he publicly stated that he wouldn't join the war, was stripped of everything including his job and heavyweight title, he never wavered from his belief.

The reason why you know Muhammad Ali's name today is because he hacked the landscape of the culture at that time. He knew how to manipulate reporters, interviewers, and journalists to get them coming back for more. He was a strategist when it came to stirring the pot and getting people riled up. A masterful boxer, he might have been a better trash-talker. Ali's brand and name will forever be ingrained in the minds of sports fans because he was who he was unapologetically and unequivocally. He was one of the prominent figures that paved the way for others to fight back and for us all to have a voice.

JOHN CARLOS

During the 1968 Olympics in Mexico City, track and field runner John Carlos along with his Olympic teammate Tommie Smith, made a public display of defiance which today still goes down as one of the most heroic acts ever done in sports. As the national anthem played, John Carlos and Tommie Smith bowed their heads and raised their black-gloved left and right fists respectively while standing upon the podium after the end of a 200-meter race. Next to them was a white Australian runner by the name of Peter Norman who didn't raise his fist, but stood alongside them in this act of courage. All of this came just months after the assassination of Martin Luther King, Jr. and Robert F. Kennedy, as well as the public police beatings at the Democratic National Convention of 1968.

Millions of people watched that day as Carlos and Smith, who won the gold and bronze medals for the US respectively, used that platform as a means to silently highlight some of the social issues and frustrations that they experienced being black in America. They saw this moment as a chance to campaign for better treatment for African Americans not only in America, but around the world. And as you can imagine this act came with a lot of repercussions.

As soon as they left the podium, they were suspended by the US Olympic committee and kicked out of Olympic Village, which is where all of the Olympians live while competing. When they got back home they faced death threats and hate mail. People called them "anti-American" and other kinds of racial slurs. They knew that this would happen. They planned for it. They instinctively knew that they'd be talked about and that their reputation would drastically be affected for the rest of their lives. But when you care about something so much that you're willing to lay everything on the line in a moment, that's when you have the ability to shape a generation and create change.

The image of John Carlos and Tommie Smith was permanently seared in the minds of the millions of people who watched that day, and now it is an iconic image for the rest of time. The Black Power Salute, as it is called today, is in books, on posters, and even in museums. It's crazy to think that a brief moment in time, one stand and one action, could be the action that cements your name in history and allows you to become the face of a movement for the rest of your life.

When you stand up for what you think is right, fair, and just, you can bend boundaries like John Carlos and Tommie Smith. You can inspire people to fight against injustice with conviction like Muhammad Ali. You can fight in the courtrooms face-to-face with legislators like Malcolm Jenkins. You can change what equal rights mean for America like Brendan Ayanbadejo. And finally, you can start a new world movement that compels the next young leaders like Colin Kaepernick.

This is not about stirring you up to join a movement or protest. This is about making sure you are firmly grounded in what you believe without wavering and understand what that's going to mean for your brand and reputation. Depending on your stance, or why you believe in what you believe in—you're going to face people who feel differently than you do. As an athlete, you're going to come across people who tell you to "Shut up and dribble" and stick to playing sports, but you know deep down inside that's not the only thing that you're about.

When you want to stand for something, stand for it. When you want to kneel for something, kneel for it. When you believe something isn't fair or right in the world, fight it with all of your heart. It'll be hard in the moment. You'll be met with criticism. Some people might stop liking you and following your brand. But at the end of the day, when you lay your head down at night, you'll know that you did the right thing. You'll be able to live with yourself and the choices that you've made. And just maybe your name and brand will be etched in history for the next generation of athletes to see and follow.

CHAPTER 10

THE IMPORTANCE
OF PHILANTHROPY

During the summer of 2018, LeBron James did something that no other athlete in history has done to my knowledge. By opening the iPromise School in his hometown of Akron, Ohio, LeBron James and his management team took philanthropy and community service to another level. Of course, not every athlete has the resources, support, or ability to pull something like this off, but that doesn't mean you shouldn't be involved or give back in some way, shape, or form.

There are a lot of athletes who pride themselves on the work that they do in underserved areas. One common initiative for athletes is to host back-to-school drives every year at the end of the summer, where they donate school supplies and backpacks. Other athletes have been known to do turkey giveaways around Thanksgiving or toy giveaways around

Christmas. Some even host free training clinics during their season. Many of them do it out of the goodness of their hearts and don't even get the acknowledgment or recognition that they deserve for the things they do.

Whatever way you personally feel is the best for you to make a difference, you shouldn't hesitate to do it. Philanthropy, especially from an athlete's perspective, is a responsibility to uplift others who aren't as fortunate as you. It is also about giving hope to the next generation, showing them that they can potentially be in the same position that you're in one day if they do the right things. When you're an athlete, giving back really isn't a choice, it's one of your main responsibilities.

When I was in college playing basketball at Niagara University, it was mandatory for us to go out and speak to kids, show face at community events, and even coach at the Special Olympics. It didn't matter how much schoolwork we had, or if we had practice or games the next day, giving back wasn't up for debate. In retrospect, it was a good thing that our coaches not only encouraged us to be active in our small community, but made us get involved in various events around the city. Though it wasn't until I got older and graduated that I understood why it was so important for us to do so.

What our coaches knew that we didn't know yet, was that as

soon as we got to that level and stepped on campus, everyone in the city would know us. As a result—the effect that we would have on other people in the surrounding area would be colossal. Just being in the room with other people could leave a life-lasting memory in their minds. And we were only low-major Division I. If you're a high-major Division I, the difference you could make is unimaginable.

So with that you have to realize that it's not so much about the number of people you impact as it is the depth of the difference you can instill. And the thing is, it doesn't even have to be in your school community. You can give back to the city or county that you grew up in. Or if you're a professional athlete you can support the city or state that you're currently playing in. Community involvement is also a really good way to start meeting more people, such as city officials and politicians throughout the city with whom you can build relationships.

Danielle Berman, founder of DB Consulting, a philanthropic consulting company for professional athletes, says that,

> Philanthropy is a great way to start a brand for athletes. While starting a nonprofit is not for every athlete, you can give back in so many ways to communities and organizations that may just want your time or support promoting an initiative. If you don't know what your passion is outside of sports, philan-

thropy projects and working in the community is a great way to make a name for yourself and learn more about what is available to you outside of sports.

Working with or supporting an initiative not only helps grow your brand, it gives you a chance to start figuring out what else you'd be interested in going forward in life. Athletes have long been known to use their platform to impact social causes, but more recently there have been a few big-name athletes who have made philanthropy a top priority when it comes to their overall brand strategy.

JJ WATT

Most NFL lineman go unrecognized and are often under-appreciated for what they do on the football field and bring to their respective teams. But JJ Watt is in a different tier altogether. What he does and gives as a professional athlete is almost irreplaceable, and as far as his contributions and causes off the football field, you could probably say the exact same thing. One of the most meaningful things he's done is leveraged social media for social causes and initiatives. JJ has been very smart and compassionate in this way as he has called out his social media following to bring awareness to different causes and issues that have affected the country.

In 2017, after Hurricane Harvey devastated cities in and

around the Gulf Coast, Watt helped raise $37 million for flood victims in his adopted hometown of Houston using a Twitter post, in addition to a viral funding campaign on the site YouCaring. His Justin J. Watt Foundation has made hundreds of smaller donations, usually a few thousand dollars, to after-school athletic programs. He also offered to pay for the funerals of the victims of the tragic shooting at a Santa Fe high school in 2018.

For JJ Watt it's clearly not just about what he can do on the football field. He's unquestionably trying to make a difference off the field. He's changing lives by using his celebrity. He's using his relationships to build and repair broken cities. He's not just talking about it on social media—he's taking action. *That* is the power of an athlete shedding light on real world problems.

"If you have the power to make someone happy, do it. The world needs more of that."

—JJ WATT

RONDA ROUSEY

Most people know Ronda Rousey for what she's been able to do in the Octagon as a UFC fighter. In 2012, she made history by becoming the first woman ever to sign with the UFC. Over and over she proved herself and dominated the sport, winning six fights in a row to defend her UFC Bantamweight title. Despite her losing to Holly Holm after her three-year reign as a champion, and dealing with constant humiliation afterward, she still put it all aside to use her recognition to do bigger things away from the sport. She's always been keen on giving back (as quiet as it's kept) and supports causes that range from mental health to world hunger. Though one of the things that she's most passionate about is young women who deal with eating disorders.

For her, it's directly tied to her own problems she had growing up. For many years she lived with bulimia and says that the reason she was able to overcome it was that she wanted to be a fighter and an inspiration to other young women. In an era where young women are expected to look perfect, or have fake bodies like so many celebrities, Rousey tells young girls to embrace the way they look, love themselves, and take care of their bodies, health wise. I think what's so important about this particular example is that Rousey used her own personal struggles to become a leader for a specific demographic of people, and she's really clear on what she hopes to accomplish and be for them.

This is obviously deeper than just building her personal brand, because her passion is a struggle that affects so many young women. It's an organic cause, because she can speak from her own experiences while being an advocate for women of all ages to eat healthy, work out, and love their bodies, regardless of size. When you're looking for causes to be part of, a good place to start looking is in your past. Think about what you've struggled with personally or have gone through that you can help other people with. That's how you find a specific group that you can speak to about your unique tribulations.

I grew up in a single-parent household and know how hard my mom had to work to raise me and my brother. I realize how many young black kids there are out there who also are being raised by their mothers independently, so one of the causes that I give back to is inner-city kids, just like me. If you can find a charity or social need that has personally affected you, it'll be that much more significant when you get involved. The more you can align with charities that support something you've personally experienced, the more you can relate to the people that support them, and the better your brand will be perceived by other people. It's a win-win scenario all the way around.

DAVID BECKHAM

David Beckham is widely respected as one of the greatest soccer players to have ever played the game. In his twenty-plus-year playing career throughout various leagues, Beckham has racked up endless awards and accolades on his way to becoming a global icon in multiple aspects of the word. Besides being a great soccer player, most people also recognize him for his looks off the field which plays into why he is a worldwide superstar and was named *People's* "Sexiest Man Alive" in 2015.

Between his many tattoos, impressive hairstyles, and over-all fashion sense, people refer to David Beckham as a model more than a soccer player. He's living proof of the well-known saying, "Men want to be like him and women want to be with him." He also has held a very strong business profile acquiring multiple endorsement deals, launching his own clothing and fragrance lines, and becoming the co-owner of soccer teams Inter Miami CF and Salford City.

Mostly because of his appearance and attractiveness, Beck-ham's brand is in the top of the top for all professional athletes. The money that he has made off the soccer field is up there with other high-level athletes such as Kobe Bryant, Tiger Woods, Tom Brady, and others who are the absolute best in their sport. But what really separates Beckham from a lot of other athletes, regardless of money or status, is his willingness to give back and make philanthropy a huge pri-ority in his life.

Many athletes might make a valiant effort to show up for appearances here and there, but Beckham is known for being a huge advocate for endless organizations and char-ities. He's not just about donating or showing up for an event or two. Beckham gets directly involved and works with the causes he's passionate about. He has supported over fifteen organizations throughout his career including African Wildlife Foundation, CHOC Children's, Elton John AIDS Foundation, Peace One Day, Raising Malawi, Red Cross, Save the Children, Save the Elephants, UNICEF, and several others.

He also has his own charity along with his wife Victoria Beckham, called the Victoria and David Beckham Charitable Trust. The focus is to provide wheelchairs to children in need. This has ultimately led to him being appointed as a UNICEF Ambassador. His efforts to give back also allowed him to receive the Global Gift Gala Philanthropist Award at the Global Gift Gala in Paris in 2013. David Beckham might appear to some people as a pretty boy athlete who only cares about playing soccer and raking in dollars, but his contributions to different organizations and the impact he's had outside of soccer speaks volumes. He is a great example of an athlete who has used his influence and brand power to bring awareness to worldwide issues he feels strongly about which will give life to a stronger legacy aside from soccer.

I think the most important thing to note about all of these examples is that philanthropy isn't something you need to highlight about yourself as an athlete. You don't do it because it looks good. You don't do it because of the highlights, media, or press. You do it because it's the right thing to do, for something that you're actually deeply fervent about. You do it because someone's life is going to be changed and they will remember that moment forever.

Some athletes might be advised by agents, publicists, or managers to work with a charity or organization because it looks good for their profile. One of the absolute worst things that you can do is pretend to support a cause because of what it can do for your image. It's the same as posting an inappropriate or unacceptable picture on Instagram because you know it'll get likes and attention. It's a short-term outlook and isn't sustainable if you want to build something that actually matters. Whether the cameras are there or not, show up and be present. In the end, people will realize what's real and what's fake. If you don't really care about making a difference, that will be apparent and eventually it will catch up with you. Never be a sell-out for the momentary gain.

CHAPTER 11

WHY SPORTS TEAMS SHOULD ENCOURAGE ATHLETES TO BUILD THEIR BRAND

For the majority of sports teams, the concept of branding is something that has been implemented for many years. Think about it. Teams such as the Boston Celtics, Los Angeles Lakers, Dallas Cowboys, and New York Yankees are world-renowned names not only because of their ability to consistently perform collectively at a high level, but also because they have consciously focused on developing reputable brands in their respective sports. Ever since I was a young kid, I've watched all of these teams perform throughout the years. A few things I have always thought to myself:

"Why is it that these particular teams hold so much more weight than other teams?"

"Why do they have so many die-hard fans and life-long followers not just in their cities but around the world?"

"Why are they constantly talked about and featured in the news and media?"

Growing up in Washington, DC, I used to wonder why there were as many—and maybe more—Dallas Cowboys fans as there were Washington Redskins fans. For a while I couldn't wrap my head around it. Then I started to think about what really makes any team great and memorable. To me, it all goes back to why any brand in the world is considered great or memorable. The most memorable teams or brands are often polarizing, invigorating, and captivating. They are revolutionary and innovative. They think differently than their competitors. They separate themselves in unique ways and evoke a certain type of emotion in people, whether that's positive or negative. They honor the ability to make people absolutely love or absolutely hate them. There's no in-between.

Most of all, they play the long-term game because they know that they will be able to build off their name forever if they do. If you dive even deeper, these teams are well-known also because of the role that the coaches and executives play in the organization. For the Boston Celtics everyone knew about coach Red Auberbach at the height of their dominance. For the Lakers, aside from the players, it was about coaches Pat Riley and Phil Jackson in addition to long-time owner Jerry Buss, who passed away in 2013. The Dallas Cowboys had coach Tom Landry, coach Bill Parcels, and team owner Jerry Jones who still to this day brings a significant amount of media attention to the team. The Yankees have gone through several notable coaches or managers over the years, some of the most famous being Yogi Berra, who was also a long-time player back in the early 1900s, and Joe Torre who was there from 1996–2007. With big name team brands, these leadership roles matter just as much as, and sometimes more than, the players on the team. But the balance between the two is usually what makes these particular teams so prevalent over time.

Putting stats aside, most people would still say that the two most successful basketball franchises in NBA history are the Boston Celtics and Los Angeles Lakers without question, right? Depending on your age, when you think of the Celtics you probably think about players like Larry Bird, Kevin McHale, Bill Russell. Or if you're a little younger you probably recall the days of Kevin Garnett, Paul Pierce, and Rajon Rondo. Although they entered the NBA in different eras, all of these players played on Celtics championship teams at one point in time. When it comes to the Lakers, I'm sure the first players that come to mind are Shaquille

O'Neal and Kobe Bryant or it might be Magic Johnson and Kareem Abdul-Jabbar. In spite of the fact that most of these athletes were well into their prime when I was young, even I'm aware of the history behind the Celtics vs. Lakers rivalry they had back then, and still have today. Their combined thirty-one NBA championships is a feat that few teams in any sport can compete with.

Back in the 80s and 90s, the Lakers were known for having players who brought a certain level of flashiness and flair to the game, a reflection of the Hollywood lifestyle. The Celtics on the other hand, brought a blue-collar attitude to the game which mirrored what the city of Boston is all about. The Lakers were all about the spotlight and showtime. The Celtics were gritty and hard-nosed. Polar opposites, but both teams wanted to do nothing more than win basketball games. Despite the overall persona of each team—at the end of the day, they were all just flat-out competitors. That contrast is a prime reason why the opposition between them made headlines repeatedly and why they are still talked about today. Even when they haven't been able to fully replicate the success, they both had throughout the 70s, 80s, 90s, and even early 2000s, people still know about their battles. Controversial themes such as good versus evil make any story play out for the better.

When you apply branding to the game of football, the Dallas Cowboys will forever be known as "America's Team."

Players like Troy Aikman, Emmitt Smith, Deion Sanders, Terrell Owens, and Michael Irwin all make up what the "Cowboys" brand has been about. The Cowboys have long been known to have some of the most compelling and contentious athletes on their team, who got it done on and off the football field, if you know what I mean.

Year after year, the Cowboys are among the most talked about NFL organizations because of the players that enter that locker room. But Jerry Jones is as competitive an owner as you'll ever find. He has owned the Cowboys since 1989 and has led them to three Super Bowl wins in total. He is one of the few team owners who actually had success playing the game as well. Combine that with his skills as a businessman and you have a guy who has turned the Cowboys brand into a multibillion-dollar entity—making them the most valuable sports team in the world at $4.8 billion.

On and off the field, the Cowboys players are in the glare of publicity probably more than other NFL players and overall, they haven't always been able to handle it well. Jerry Jones has taken risks on several players who ended up getting into legal trouble. From drug abuse to sexual assault allegations, the Cowboys locker room is typically filled with drama and various predicaments. But at the same time, that's what makes their brand so legendary. They play the "bad guy" and they completely own it. They welcome guys who often carry troubled pasts and put them at the forefront of the organization, despite any outsider's opinion. That's exactly what makes the Cowboys, the Cowboys.

And lastly, talking about baseball, the New York Yankees is a team you know about regardless of whether you're a fan or not. If you're American, then you know something about the Yankees' storied history. Baseball is the national pastime; it is the oldest professional sport in America. Most people would probably think that the Yankees started when baseball started, but they actually aren't even one of the top-ten oldest teams in Major League Baseball. They've just been the best and most consistent since their inception.

From Babe Ruth and Lou Gehrig to Derek Jeter and Alex Rodriguez, the Yankees are easily the most respected baseball organization of all time. Starting with Murderer's Row (nickname of the Yankees baseball team in the late 1920s) until now, they've always had incredible players who placed winning the World Series above everything. Baseball isn't baseball without the New York Yankees. They are the kings of the game and relish being in the spotlight and in one of the greatest cities on this planet.

All of the players on these teams throughout these sports, whether consciously or subconsciously, have built individual brands whose perception extended to the teams they played for, but what they all became known for was having a winning tradition. An athlete's brand can be enthralling and exciting, but over time it will never work as best as it can if you don't win games and championships. These teams will forever be etched in fans' minds because of their ability to consistently compete at the highest levels and because of the players that played for them in past years who were often unpredictable, problematic, yet captivating.

Here are several reasons why every single sports team from high school up to professional, should be encouraging every athlete on the team to build their personal brand:

It brings exposure back to the team. Everything an athlete does on or off the playing field is a reflection of the organization that they play for. Regardless of whether this is seen as a good thing or a bad thing, it's the reality. And if you have high-character players, it would do a lot of good for the team if they knew how to manage their personal brand. If an athlete has a foundation, there is room for collaboration with the organization and all of that publicity adds positive value back to the team. If an athlete does any major or influential work in the community, that just spreads awareness to what the team is doing overall.

The more that teams encourage their athletes to get involved and build their brands in the respective communities they play in, the more this will translate into brand loyalty and ticket sales for the team long term.

Players are more relevant and noticeable to the fans. In the digital age, there are a lot of athletes that have become more popular than the teams that they play for, especially on social media. With players having very large fan bases, team executives, coaches, and representatives can leverage the player's relevance to execute campaigns, elevate the team's brand, and promote team events/activities. Capitalizing on a player's relevance and popularity is the easiest way to grow a new fan base and/or expand into different markets. Most colleges already utilize this tactic by using student-athletes' image and likeness on marketing material and posters.

It teaches players about career longevity and post-career planning. Obviously, once a player retires, they have to start another career doing something else. If they start building their brand during their career it will help them figure out what to do next. What most team executives and coaches don't understand is that a personal brand can help players start to think about who they are and what they want to do when they're done. Instead of being a distraction, brand building enhances an athlete's play and focus, because they're not being one-dimensional.

If teams inspire athletes to do this, we'll see more players have better and more effective transitions into life after sports, which can equal less backlash on teams and leagues, plus greater outcomes for future athletes who play for them.

It teaches players about what it takes to maintain a public image. The more that teams talk about how players should conduct themselves in public and in front of the media, the more likely players will conduct themselves appropriately. Teams and organizations who truly care will help athletes understand this, because they know that it will be a reflection of their character, and who they will be ten years from now.

There is a lot of good that can come from a team preaching the importance of brand building to their athletes. Teams and organizations should reiterate to athletes that the foundation of branding is about people, character, and relationships, not logos and posting cool pictures online or having a clean website. All of the rest of the design and pretentious stuff comes much later after the infrastructure is set in stone. Teams now have no choice but to educate and empower athletes to grow their brands, because athletes hold way more power at the professional level—even at the college level—than they did years ago. As an athlete, you are in an incredible position to dictate your reputation along with the team you play for by your actions.

That was one of the first things that I realized when I got to college. Everything I did, whether bad or good, was an example of what our team was about. It was an example of our culture and how people saw us as a whole. I understood right away that having this control as an athlete could be a positive or negative thing, whichever way I or any one of my teammates decided to take it. This is why organizations and institutions have to first invest in athletes who have a high level of integrity before a high level of talent. When a player makes a positive impact, it reflects well on the organization or institution that player was associated with. But when they do something bad, the negative implications for a university or team organization can impede recruiting, introduce actions, and put a black cloud over a team for years to come.

No matter who you are, you cannot hide in today's world. Who you really are will come to the surface sooner or later. Your personal life as an employed athlete or student-athlete, otherwise known as the brand that you have outside of your day job, is still a representation of the company or team you work with or for. You carry your coworkers, teammates, coaches, and organization on your back everywhere you go.

Athletes, universities, and top-level franchises alike have to take this into consideration because this is exactly what we are living through today. If an athlete does right by the team, everyone wins. When they do wrong, everybody—and I mean every single person in the organization or athletic department—fails in one way or another.

While I was in college, one of my teammates got hit with a DUI case; another teammate and I were passengers in the vehicle. The other passenger and I were not arrested, but my teammate who was driving was. The very next day when our coaches found out, the entire team paid for it. And we didn't all just pay for it by running sprints the entire practice until we passed out, but we all suffered the consequences as a team in the local newspaper. It goes to show that when one does wrong, we all do wrong.

So at the end of the day, you have to realize that athlete branding is much more about the faces we see in our feeds that slow our scroll on social media. It's not as much about the logos, universities, or companies as it's been in the past. Logos don't sign autographs or win games. Athletes do. The more that teams and organizations realize that this is the key, the more intentional they will be about empowering and educating athletes about branding off the playing field, and the better off they'll all be further down the line.

CHAPTER 12

BUILDING A LEGACY AND ELEVATING YOUR BRAND IN LIFE AFTER SPORTS

Most of everything you'll need to know about branding is laid out here. By reading this book, I hope you now have most of the knowledge and the foundation for long-term brand success as an athlete. But if you're reading this and you're completely done playing or on your way toward retirement, you might be thinking, "How do I leverage my personal brand as a former athlete?" "How do I scale, grow, and manage my brand five, ten, or even fifteen years down the line?" "How can I maintain a strong fanbase and the attention that I've accumulated over the years?" These are all real and valid concerns, so now we're going to dive into how you can create a legacy in life after sports.

Throughout this book, I've mentioned a lot of different athletes from different generations. Athletes such as Michael Jordan, Magic Johnson, Alex Rodriguez, and others who have maintained and kept their relevance for years after they were done playing the game. As I have gone deeper into what an athlete's brand requires, questions such as, "How are these particular athletes able to do this?" and "Why do people still know their name and why do people still care about them over other athletes who might have been just as good?" began to arise. I know that these are big-name athletes; they are some of the best in their respective sports. But whether you're the top of the top or barely known, the process and strategy is still the same to maintain relevance for the long term.

For the most part, it comes down to finding ways to elevate your personal brand and doing things that are going to take it to the next level each and every year. It comes down to you staying on the public's radar, and doing things that are actually worth talking about. The athletes mentioned above are some of the greatest of their generation, but there have been a ton of athletes who weren't the greatest, and still are talked about today because they maintained that relevance long after their career was over.

The athletes who weren't the best or most talented, that still are being talked about after retirement, are being talked about because they are doing things that garner attention, or things that can produce a good story. They didn't retire, kick their feet up, and say, "I had a pretty good career, now I can chill." Even if that's what they wanted to do, most of them couldn't because they didn't make enough money to do so. Competitors will be competitors so in most cases, these athletes now go harder in life after sports than they did as an athlete.

Complacency is the enemy of progress.

Retirement as an athlete is not the same as regular retirement. You have to keep pushing and doing things that you're passionate about, not only to make money, but to also continuing building on what you had when you were an athlete. You have to put yourself in a position to be as successful, if not more successful, as you were as an athlete. You simply have to create things, do something, or be someone that people want to focus on.

ATHLETES WHO HAVE ELEVATED THEIR BRAND AFTER THEY RETIRED

Being retired doesn't necessarily mean that your brand has to retire or even that your fanbase goes away. If you're an athlete with a significant online and digital presence, you can keep your fans interested in you for a very long time. The carryover is that people will now keep you top of mind even though you are retired.

Below are a few key examples of former professional athletes who actually built stronger brands once they walked away from their sport. And a few of them you might not have even paid attention to when they were playing. This shows you that no matter what you want to transition into in life after sports, your brand as an athlete can take you a long way.

JUSTIN FORSETT

He was once known for being a stand-out running back for the NFL team the Baltimore Ravens, but since he has retired, he has begun to gain recognition for what he's doing as an entrepreneur and speaker. As the co-founder of the company ShowerPill, Justin Forsett along with his two co-founders Wendell Hunter and Wale Forrester, who also played football at a high level, gained nationwide attention when they pitched to investors on *Shark Tank*, an entrepreneurial-themed reality show. They have also been featured on ABC News and have gotten their product in retailers such as Walmart in just a few years after its formation.

The idea for ShowerPill, which is a premium wipe that works like a disposable washcloth, was born while the three co-founders were in school together at UC Berkeley. They didn't have a lot of time to shower between classes, football practice, and other activities and needed something as a substitute solution to supplement their hygiene. So they designed a product to scratch their own itch. Justin's brand in particular has exploded largely due to the fact that he is the most well-known founder of the company, due to his NFL longevity. Furthermore, he has also taken steps to do other things outside of growing the company.

Among those things include side-line reporting, public speaking, participating on podcasts, using Instagram to post motivational messages, and even attending a class at Harvard Business School. He also has a huge presence on Twitter and regularly engages with fans in discussions around football. I love the way Justin has transitioned his brand over from being just a football player. He has a clear understanding of the power of his personal brand and how his legacy as an athlete can be leveraged to build and grow his next passion, ShowerPill. Because Justin does other things outside of ShowerPill to build his name, his company will directly benefit from it monetarily while framing a legacy for himself going forward in life.

EMMANUEL ACHO

This is a name that you might not be familiar with, but the way that he has grown exponentially as a retired athlete is something to take note of. Emmanuel Acho is a former NFL linebacker who played for the Cleveland Browns and Philadelphia Eagles. He has parlayed his average NFL career into becoming one of the nation's youngest sports analysts as of 2019, which won him a *Forbes* "30 Under 30" award in the same year.

His brand and personality also transcend football due to his relationship with Yvonne Orji, one of the stars of the hit HBO show, *Insecure*. Another claim to fame actually came through Twitter, an outlet that he is extremely active on and has about 50,000 followers at the time of writing.

In January of 2015, he was contacted by a young girl named Hannah Delmonte who asked him to escort her to prom if she could get 2,000 retweets on Twitter about their conversation. He upped it to 10,000 tweets and in about three hours that goal was met. About a month or so later, Emmanuel actually took some time off from finishing up school at the University of Texas to fly to Purcellville, Virginia, to meet Hannah in person and accept her prom invitation. He also gave her an autographed jersey which said, "Prom 15" on it and from there, the story went viral and made national news.

This story is unique and important for several reasons. Emmanuel displayed an act of great character by simply doing what he said he was going to do, and being a man of his word. That is a major part of branding. He built an incredible amount of trust and connection with the fanbase he already had by doing this. The icing on top was that it helped him go viral, which exposed his brand to even more people. People saw him as personable and more than just a famous athlete. At that moment he became just a good, everyday person, who just happens to be an athlete.

That experience was major for him and was the springboard for future opportunities that he's had. To really solidify how good a person he is, Emmanuel is not just an analyst for ESPN now, but he is also heavily involved in a non-profit called Living Hope Christian Ministries which focuses on bringing doctors to Nigeria, his homeland. Emmanuel didn't have a very long NFL career, but will be able to have a successful career outside of the game because he knows the importance of using his name and brand for good.

LISA LESLIE

Lisa Leslie is regarded as one of the most recognized and talented female athletes of all time. Coming out of high school, she was the top basketball recruit in the nation and decided to stay home to attend the University of Southern California, where she won college player of the year several times. After finishing up there, she then went on to play in the 1996 Olympics where she won a gold medal. This was right before the inaugural season of the WNBA. The following year she was signed to her hometown team, the Los Angeles Sparks, the team that she would go on to play with during her entire professional career.

In 2002, she became the first woman to dunk in the WNBA, which basically certified her as a legit athlete in everyone's eyes. Women hoopers are dunking frequently now, but before Lisa did it, it was unheard of. Lisa retired in 2009 after a twelve-year pro career, winning endless awards such as three-time MVP, two-time Finals MVP, two-time WNBA Champion, eight-time WNBA All-Star, and three-time WNBA All-Star Game MVP. But the impressive thing was that Leslie's brand had taken off before she even took her last dribble. She was and still is an inspiration to young female athletes worldwide.

Since her retirement she has plunged into several other ventures and opportunities that she's passionate about. She's been able to capitalize on her figure as a tall, fit athlete to pursue modeling and acting gigs. Not only has she been featured in *Vogue Magazine*, and on the cover of *ESPN*, she's acted in tv shows such as *Sister Sister*, *The Game*, *Superstar*, *The Simpsons,* and *One on One*. She's also been in movies such as *Think Like A Man* and *Uncle Drew*. While doing all of this, Leslie is also a commentator and sports analyst. She's been featured on networks such as NBC, FOX Sports, ABC, and KABC-TV LA. Not to mention she's pursuing these things while being a mother of two.

Everything she's been able to do is incredible, but the most remarkable thing that she's done in her post-playing career is to become part owner of the Los Angeles Sparks, the team she once starred on. How many athletes do you know who own a piece of the team that they once played on? I bet not many. All the things that she has been able to do outside of the game have been based on the impact that she wants to have on young women, her faith, and how she's held herself to such a high standard throughout the years.

Rarely do you find an African American female athlete who has been able to change the lives of people from all different cultures, ethnicities, and backgrounds. Lisa Leslie has done that using the game of basketball. When you talk about the WNBA, you have to mention Lisa and what she has done for the female athletes who have come after her. Leslie is a scholar, a leader, an executive, an entrepreneur, a mother, a visionary, and lastly an athlete. That's how you build a brand that lasts well after your playing days are over.

BARON DAVIS

Baron Davis is easily one of the most electrifying and explosive point guards to ever play the game of basketball. In my opinion, he's one of the most underrated as well. He was drafted as the third overall pick in the 1999 NBA draft out of UCLA, so everyone knew he was poised to be a big-name star in the league. It was just a matter of when it would happen. Though growing up it didn't always seem like that would be the case. Baron came up in a rough neighborhood in central Los Angeles and saw drugs and gang violence every single day.

Because of his academic smarts and athletic ability, he was able to gain a scholarship to Crossroads High School in Santa Monica, where he had to mix and mingle with the kids of celebrities and high-net-worth families. That gave him a different perspective on life and where he could go if he stayed focused and worked hard. So that's exactly what he did. He worked on his game and stayed in the books which afforded him a scholarship to UCLA, and then gave him the opportunity to make the leap to the league.

Throughout his thirteen-year NBA career, he had his fair share of ups and downs, and injuries, but what always stayed consistent was his business savvy and the opportunities that he took advantage of off the court. In what might have been a controversial move at the time, Baron fired his agent very early in his NBA career and instead enlisted one of his former teammates, Todd Ramasar, to represent him and his endeavors off the court, even though Todd had just gotten his law degree and barely had any experience representing or managing players. Nonetheless, Baron was a visionary. He saw it differently. He knew where he was going with this.

Baron saw an opportunity to give his former college teammate a shot at partnering with him to build a brand that extended beyond basketball, even though Todd was only twenty-three years old at the time. They both were extremely young, but Baron and Todd took their street smarts, combined with business acumen, to land some lucrative deals off the court including gaining some equity stake in Vitamin Water which was sold to Coca-Cola for $4.1 billion in 2007. That deal was only the beginning of what was to come for Baron Davis who is now a serial entrepreneur, investor, and film producer.

So far, he's been able to leverage his stage as a basketball player to create a multitude of opportunities which expand his impact as a leader in the community of athletes. I once had the opportunity to meet and talk to Baron for a few minutes, and immediately I could tell that he thought differently than other people. He was an out-of-the-box type guy, and that mindset has contributed to how much success he's had in life after basketball. Many people look to Baron not because of who he was as an athlete, but because of the stories he has been able to tell about where he comes from and the difference he has been able to make for people in the Los Angeles community. It's not often that you see a young black athlete from central Los Angeles not only make it to the professional ranks of sports, but also be able to use that platform as a means to give back to the world around him. Baron Davis is that athlete.

GEORGE FOREMAN

George Forman used to be known for wreaking havoc in the ring. As the once two-time heavyweight champion and Olympic gold medalist, his boxing legacy was already bound to be fixed in the history of the sport, but what's been even more awe-inspiring is what he has been able to do outside of the ring with his name and brand. I'd be amazed to come across someone who hasn't heard of, seen, or used the George Foreman Grill before. The craziest thing is that most people probably don't even know that George Foreman wasn't even the person who initially came up with the idea!

It was originally created in 1994 by a man named Michael W. Boehm, a lifelong inventor who worked for a company called Tsann Kuen USA. While there are some mixed facts about who first owned the rights to sell the grill and what the earliest name of it was, it wasn't until George Foreman got involved that it really took off. Salton Inc. ultimately acquired the rights to manufacture and market the two-sided, hinged grill and successfully brought Foreman on as its celebrity endorser. The story gets even more interesting as it is reported that George Foreman almost passed up on the deal when it was first brought to him. He wasn't even interested in it, calling it a "toy" when he saw it. It wasn't until his wife used it and cooked him a burger that his mind changed completely. The taste, and the grease being removed from it, convinced him that it was worth his time to invest in.

He then called up his partners, and said, "I'm going to do

that deal." In exchange for promoting it and putting his face on the brand, Foreman received about 40 percent of the profits for each grill sold and the rest is history. It is estimated that he has since made over $300 million dollars from the profits for the grill. About 2.5 times what he earned during his career as a boxer. Now, the Foreman name will forever be remembered not necessarily for boxing, but for a product that will continue to be in the homes of millions and millions of people worldwide. It just goes to show you that when you build your brand not just for your athletic career, but as an athlete who knows they will one day walk away from the game, it's amazing what types of things can come into your life.

BEING AN ATHLETE ENDS, BUT BRANDING IS FOREVER

I realize that reading all of this information has been a lot to take in and comprehend. Keep in mind that you won't pick up on all of this in one day and also that building a brand takes plenty of persistence and consistency. When Phil Knight started Nike (originally called Blue Ribbon Sports) in 1964, he never imagined that it would become the mega-brand that it is today. In fact, he often talks about how close the company was to being bankrupt multiple times in his book, *Shoe Dog*. He just played the long game and believed in what he was building.

Building a brand, like anything in life, is a game of peaks

and valleys. Highs and lows. Ups and downs. But it's nothing you haven't already experienced being an athlete. You'll have good days and days in which you just aren't feeling it. This is the same thing you'll experience while building your platform. Contrary to what you see or believe, overnight successes really do take ten years, if even you don't see the underlying workings.

I think about what LeBron James has been able to accomplish at what seems like such a young age, but then I remember that most of his ventures and ideas have been in motion since his NBA career first started. He didn't just start companies yesterday and they became what they are now. Although he had the name, the money, the team, and the resources, these things have happened over years and years of consistent work, strategizing, and implementation.

I tell athletes that I come across that they should wholeheartedly embrace the journey, on and off the playing field. Being an elite-level athlete, or even just an athlete in general, is an experience that very few people get a chance to have. People want to be like you. People look up to you and what you're able to do. You're inspiring because you've fought through adversity, you've chased your passion, and you've sacrificed. You've also performed for something bigger than yourself and most of all you've given hope to others that anything can be done if you set your mind to it. Your story and brand will last well beyond the game you play, if you take the right steps. The steps that you take off of the court or field will give you experiences outside of being an athlete that you never thought you would have.

When you're done being an athlete, it's not the end of the journey, it's the beginning of the rest of your life. When you look at Kobe Bryant in retirement, you see that he's hoping to make an impact beyond his athletic abilities with his brand and company, Granity Studios. When you see Derek Jeter, he's hoping to inspire other people and athletes to do greater things with his companies. When you see Peyton Manning, you see that he's living his other passions and expanding on his career outside of being a Hall of Fame quarterback through endorsements and appearances. Even older athletes such as Dave Bing and Junior Bridgman, who both played in the NBA during the 70s, have built brands that extend into politics and fast food franchising respectively.

There's no limit to your ambition. The athletes who create a brand, a new identity outside of their sport, are the ones who transition effectively and adequately. The athletes you see who are successful after the game, no matter how big or small they were during their athletic career, used their brand and influence to create a new career once they transitioned. Your legacy as an athlete matters, but what you're able to do outside of it is way more important. Sports is only a game at the end of the day. In every situation, it's just a means to an end.

When you reach the end of your career and look back at it all, trust me, you're going to think a lot about your regrets. You're going to think about what you did wrong and what you wish you would have done way more than you think about your accomplishments and achievements. Some regrets are going to be there regardless, but don't let not taking advantage of your brand be one of those things. It doesn't matter whether you retire ten years from now, or tomorrow. Don't let your story go to waste. I dare you to be the influence that the world needs you to be. I implore you to be the example that the next generation of athletes needs you to be. And last but not least, don't ever let anyone tell you that you can't be more than an athlete.

ABOUT THE AUTHOR

MALCOLM LEMMONS is a former professional athlete turned entrepreneur and author. During his days playing basketball overseas, Malcolm didn't know how to prepare for life after sports. He began to write about his experiences and obstacles in his athletic career, which led to his first book, *Lessons from the Game*. Malcolm has also written for Huffington Post, Athlete Network, and Kulture Hub, and has been featured on MLB Network and Front Office Sports. You can learn more at malcolmlemmons.com and follow him on Instagram and Twitter @malcolmlemmons.

Made in United States
Orlando, FL
08 November 2023

38726025R00129